Teacher Evaluation

TO ENHANCE PROFESSIONAL PRACTICE

Charlotte Danielson & Thomas L. McGreal

Association for Supervision and Curriculum Development
Alexandria, Virginia USA

Educational Testing Service
Princeton, New Jersey USA

Association for Supervision and Curriculum Development
1703 N. Beauregard St. • Alexandria, VA 22311-1714 USA
Telephone: 1-800-933-2723 or 703-578-9600 • Fax: 703-575-5400
Web site: http://www.ascd.org • E-mail: member@ascd.org

Educational Testing Service
Rosedale Road
Princeton, NJ 08541-0001
Telephone: 609-734-5555
Fax: 609-734-5450
Web site: http://www.teachingandlearning.org

ASCD Staff

Gene R. Carter, *Executive Director*
Michelle Terry, *Associate Executive Director,*
   Program Development
Nancy Modrak, *Director, Publishing*
John O'Neil, *Director of Acquisitions*
Julie Houtz, *Managing Editor of Books*
Carolyn R. Pool, *Associate Editor*
Ernesto Yermoli, *Project Assistant*

Gary Bloom, *Director, Design and Production Services*
Karen Monaco, *Senior Designer*
Kimberly Lau, *Designer*
Tracey A. Smith, *Production Manager*
Dina Murray Seamon, *Production Coordinator*
Cynthia Stock, *Desktop Publisher*
Winfield Swanson, *Indexer*

Printed in the United States of America.

July 2000 member book (pc). ASCD Premium, Comprehensive, and Regular members periodically receive ASCD books as part of their membership benefits. No. FY00-08.

ASCD Product No. 100219
ASCD member price: $20.95   nonmember price: $24.95

Library of Congress Cataloging-in-Publication Data
Danielson, Charlotte.
  Teacher evaluation to enhance professional practice / Charlotte Danielson and Thomas L. McGreal.
     p. cm.
Includes bibliographical references and index.
"ASCD product no. 100219"—T.p. verso.
   ISBN 0-87120-380-4 (quality pbk.)
   1. Teachers—Rating of—United States. 2. Teaching—United States—Evaluation. I. McGreal, Thomas L. II. Title.
   LB2838 .D26 2000
   371.14'4—dc21   00-009116

06 05 04 03 02   10 9 8 7 6 5 4 3

Teacher Evaluation to Enhance Professional Practice

List of Figures

Prologue: A Tale of Two People

Karen closes her plan book with a sigh. "This is so *stupid!*" Her formal observation is scheduled for the day after tomorrow, and she has the pre-observation conference in a few minutes. As she walks down the hall, she thinks about how she will talk about her lesson. She knows she won't mention that she picked this particular lesson because it fits nicely into the categories on the district's evaluation form (a stupid form, she thinks), but one on which she can look good. Also, it is a lesson she has done many times in the past, so there are unlikely to be any surprises with the students. So, although she is a little nervous, she is fairly certain she doesn't really have anything to worry about.

Anyway, what does her principal know? He was a high school science teacher before becoming an assistant principal at the middle school and then principal of the elementary school. He has never taught 4th graders, doesn't know how they think, what all the new curriculum initiatives are. Karen has some genuine challenges in her class: how to integrate the three students with limited English proficiency; how to teach the new "inquiry" math program; how to run a writers' workshop. But she won't try any of these in her evaluation lesson: What's the point? Something would be bound to go wrong, and who needs it? Anyway, the principal probably thinks that kids should be quiet and in their seats in a "good" lesson.

The point of this evaluation exercise is just to get through it.

❧ ❧ ❧

Charles is sitting in his office, waiting for Karen to arrive. He lets his eyes wander out of the window, and wishes he could just skip this whole evaluation process. It's so pointless—he and the teachers play out their assigned roles, and yet nothing really happens. And it takes so much time! He has 30 teachers to evaluate, and each one has to be observed twice during the year. When you add it up—60 observations and 120 conferences, plus the write-ups on top of it—he devotes about 135 hours a year to evaluation. And for what? To put a piece of paper in the personnel file in June!

What's more, he pretty much knows now what the pieces of paper will say; he could practically write them now. Everyone will receive a "satisfactory" rating in everything. He knows how the game is played; he was a teacher himself only a few years ago. Do the safe thing. Don't rock the boat. And even if he has serious concerns about a teacher, his hands are tied. The last time a teacher was dismissed for incompetence, it took four years and huge legal bills. The superintendent has made it clear that she does not have the stomach for much of that.

1

And yet, a lot is going on in the district. It is suddenly really important to improve student achievement on the state tests. The school is implementing a couple of new programs that Charles thinks hold great promise. But when does he have time to really discuss these with teachers? So much of his time is consumed with noninstructional matters in the first place: meeting with parent groups, attending administrative meetings, preparing budgets, troubleshooting with the school secretary and the custodian. What little time he does have for "instruction" is taken up with these stupid evaluations!

☛ ☛ ☛

Karen and Charles are caught in the annual cycle of teacher evaluation, an activity that purports to support professional growth, but that does not and cannot. Most educators agree that they could use a better system, but have not been able to devote sustained energy to creating one. This book, we hope, will offer them some guidance.

1

A Flawed System

As the Prologue shows, the experiences of Karen and Charles—and many other teachers and administrators—signal some of the pervasive problems with today's teacher evaluation systems. Though well intentioned, these systems are burdensome and not helpful for teachers who are looking to improve their practice. Nor do they assist administrators in making difficult decisions regarding teacher performance. We see six main areas of deficiency in current teacher evaluation systems.

What's Wrong?

Outdated, Limited, Evaluative Criteria

Many evaluation systems in use today were developed in the early to mid-1970s and reflect what educators believed about teaching at that time. Current systems rely heavily on the documentation of a small number of "observable behaviors," such as "writing the learning objectives on the board," "smiling at students as you greet them," and the like. Hence, Karen will be sure, in her observed lesson, to do all the things she "should" do, so Charles can check them off on his list.

This generation of evaluation systems is grounded in the conception of teaching that prevailed in the 1970s, and many are based on the work originally done by Madeline Hunter (e.g., *Mastery Teaching*, 1982). The research on student learning that accompanied these systems relied on the only available measures of student achievement: norm-referenced, machine-scorable, multiple-choice tests of fairly low-level knowledge. But our goals for student achievement have evolved—we are now interested in more complex learning, in problem-solving, in the application of knowledge to unfamiliar situations. Further, recent educational research, particularly on the nature of the brain and how it learns, has made it clear that we need new approaches to teaching and, therefore, to the description and evaluation of teaching.

This is not an indictment of earlier models; indeed, they represented the best of what was known at the time. Like other professions, however, education is built around a conception of practice based on current and emerging research findings; as those findings suggest new approaches, pedagogical practices must also move forward.

Therefore, because educational research has advanced over the past 25 years, and classroom practice is following suit, the evaluation of teaching must reflect these newer techniques. The evaluative criteria used should represent the most current research available; and we need to make provisions, as time goes on, to revise those criteria to reflect current findings. For example, teachers might be asked to demonstrate that their students are successfully achieving the state's content standards, or that they are teaching for understanding (rather than merely rote learning).

Few Shared Values and Assumptions About Good Teaching

As the conception of learning and hence good teaching has gradually shifted from a "behaviorist" to a more "constructivist" view, in line with emerging research, many educators have developed their own personal views of what constitutes good practice. In some cases, teachers have been more inclined to embrace the new approaches than have been their administrators; in other cases, the reverse has been true. Karen is not sure what Charles considers a good lesson; she is inclined to play it safe and keep the students in their seats during the observation. The system in place in the school does not leave room for discussion of these matters. In any event, Karen and Charles have never discussed this; for all either of them knows, they might agree on a more complex view of teaching than that reflected in their evaluation form.

But the district has never forged a common language to describe teaching, one on which everyone in the district can agree. Nor does the district's evaluation system support teachers and administrators' having professional conversations that would be a learning experience. As a result, teachers can only guess at the values and assumptions about good teaching on which their performance will be judged.

Lack of Precision in Evaluating Performance

Most evaluation systems depend on a single dichotomous scale, such as "satisfactory," "needs improvement," and the like. Some evaluation systems, on the other hand, have attempted to incorporate "rating scales," that is, scales from "1" to "4" or levels representing "low, medium, and high," or "needs improvement, satisfactory, and outstanding," or "seldom, frequently, and always," or similar headings. Though offering a promise of greater objectivity and specificity than a simple checklist of whether certain behaviors were observed or not, such systems typically fall well short of their potential, because there is little agreement on what constitutes a "level 3," or "medium," or "satisfactory" performance. That is, one person's "satisfactory" might be another person's "outstanding." We don't have, in other words, the equivalent of the "anchor papers" or "benchmarks" used in evaluating student work against rubrics.

Further, several factors prevent the full use of the rating scale, if one exists. First, given the culture surrounding evaluation in many school environments, most teachers expect to receive all "outstandings" on their evaluations, regardless of the actual quality of their teaching and the definition of "outstanding." Anything less, particularly for experienced teachers, would signal a serious deficiency. This has come to be known as the "Lake Wobegon Effect," named for Garrison Keillor's (1985) fictional town in Minnesota where "all the children are above average." Second, in some school districts, administrators are reluctant to be completely honest in their evaluations of teaching.

Occasionally, an administrator concludes that a teacher is not functioning well in the current school but may believe that the teacher could perform successfully in a different environment. Alternatively, a principal may not honestly believe that a teacher could perform any more successfully in another school, but would like that teacher removed from her staff without enduring the trauma of a dismissal. A transfer will be difficult to arrange, however, and will be difficult to sell to the other administrator, if the teacher has received poor evaluations. Hence, many administrators are less than candid in their assessments of teaching; in their hopes of having the teacher transferred to another school, they will write a positive evaluation. This practice is sometimes dubbed "the dance of the lemons."

Finally, in many situations, teachers have little trust in the ratings given. Although all teachers want the highest rating, and believe that their careers will be damaged if they don't receive it, they believe that administrators reserve the highest ratings for their friends or protégés. The integrity of the entire process, then, may be seriously compromised by a perception of favoritism.

Hierarchical, One-Way Communication

Most evaluation systems are characterized by top-down communication, in which the only evidence of teacher performance is that collected by an administrator during classroom observations. Typically, a principal or other supervisor conducts an observation, takes notes, writes up the observation, and provides feedback to the teacher on her performance. In the absence of clear evaluative criteria, this feedback is likely to be highly idiosyncratic, and may or may not be of value to the teacher.

Further, depending on the relationship between the school district and the teachers' association, the climate surrounding evaluation may be essentially negative, with a prevailing perception on the part of teachers that the real purpose of the exercise is one of "gotcha," in which administrators look for opportunities to find fault. But even when the climate is positive, the teacher's role is essentially passive; thus the teachers don't *do* anything.

No Differentiation Between Novice and Experienced Practitioners

Teaching, alone among the professions, makes the same demands on novices as on experienced practitioners. The moment first-year teachers enter their first classrooms, they are held to the same standard—and subjected to the same procedures—as their more experienced colleagues.

Most other professions build in a period of apprenticeship. No one would expect a prospective surgeon, straight from medical school, to take charge of a complex operation. Nor would a new architect be asked to design, single-handedly, a large office building. Yet the job of teaching for a novice is identical to that of a seasoned veteran (sometimes harder); and the procedures used to evaluate them are identical. When the principal arrives to conduct an observation of a novice teacher, she holds the very same checklist as that used for experienced teachers.

It is important to remember, however, that from the standpoint of the public, it is not unreasonable to expect a skilled level of teaching in every classroom. After all, a student should not receive an inferior education just because he or she is assigned to the class of an inexperienced teacher. The school district's implied contract with the public ensures that all teachers exhibit at least a certain level of skill.

In the case of teachers, the state's responsibility (through its licensing procedures) ends with the guarantee of minimum competence; after that, it is the role of each school district, through its procedures for teacher evaluation and professional growth, to ensure excellence. And it is in everyone's collective interest that all teachers perform at a high level; teachers in a school, even more than architects in a firm, work as a team to ensure the learning of all students in that school. Although the school district must ensure that all teachers (including beginning teachers) have at least a certain level of skill, the procedures used might be somewhat different for novices than for their more experienced colleagues.

Limited Administrator Expertise

Many teachers are more expert regarding their work than the administrators who "supervise" them—more knowledgeable about their discipline, current pedagogical approaches, or the developmental characteristics of the students they teach. Many administrators, especially those whose background is in the humanities, would be hard-pressed to spot content inaccuracies in a chemistry class. Similarly, administrators' knowledge of introducing equivalent fractions to 4th graders, or developing writing skills, may be weak; and they may not be familiar with the proper use (or possible misuse) of graphing calculators in a mathematics classroom.

It is true that all teaching environments share important characteristics, and that a thoughtful and well-trained observer can recognize these characteristics (or their absence)

in a variety of settings. But knowledge of content, of content-related pedagogy, and the approaches to learning displayed by students at different developmental levels, are highly relevant to teaching. Teachers may well be more knowledgeable in these matters than the administrator who evaluates their performance; this fact undermines the evaluation process, contributing to the perception that it has little value. As the Prologue makes clear, Karen does not expect to learn anything useful from Charles as a result of his observation and evaluation of her lesson—indeed, she believes, perhaps rightly, that his knowledge of 4th graders and their learning is virtually nonexistent.

The Result?

A combination of these factors—limited administrator expertise, little shared understanding of what constitutes good teaching, low levels of trust between teachers and administrators—lead to a culture of passivity and protection. Teachers are unlikely to be honest about any difficulties they may be experiencing if they fear that "problems" will be described on the final evaluation document as "deficiencies." Such an atmosphere is not a safe one for taking risks; the culture surrounding evaluation is not one of professional inquiry. Moreover, because teachers may not honestly respect the administrator's expertise and, therefore, do not expect to learn from the evaluation process, they have little incentive for admitting to difficulties that may only be held against them. In addition, the feeling that "nothing can be done" saps energy from other projects within the school that require people to think in new ways.

Thus, we see Karen doing what's near-universal in schools: She performs a "canned" lesson for the evaluation observation, a lesson designed to demonstrate all the "behaviors" on the checklist and one in which the students may have been coached before the observation. This may be the same lesson that was taught for the past five years of observations, and it may be a good lesson. But the administrator is unlikely to learn anything about the teacher that he did not know previously, and the subsequent conversation is unlikely to be professionally rewarding for either the teacher or the administrator.

Because of the factors described here—unclear or inappropriate evaluative criteria, limited administrative expertise, one-way communication—current teacher evaluation is a meaningless exercise. It yields little of value to either the teachers or the schools in which they work, simultaneously feeling like a "gotcha" to the teachers while consuming a great deal of administrator time. Some of these reasons are structural; some are cultural. But either way, neither Karen nor Charles will derive much benefit from participating in the ritual called "evaluation."

Of course, it can be worse. In some situations, the culture surrounding teacher evaluation is so poisoned that there is no trust between teachers and administrators; and teachers believe that administrators use the evaluation system to get rid of people they dislike. The system itself can contribute to this phenomenon, if administrator judgments need not be based on specific evidence, if the system does not permit teachers to present their interpretation of events, and if the environment surrounding evaluation does not permit genuine and professional conversation about teaching. If a system allows an administrator to dole out low ratings, with no justification and no opportunity for teachers to respond in a substantive manner, the system is worse than meaningless; it is punitive and damaging.

School districts have little incentive, however, to change the situation. After all, except where the atmosphere is truly poisoned, no one (none of the adults, at least) is being harmed by the evaluation practices in place. People go through the motions, they follow the procedures, and there is a piece of paper to put in the human resources file at the end of the year. The ritual is essentially meaningless, with little good resulting from it. We believe educators can design better systems.

First Principles: Why Teacher Evaluation?

Virtually every public school district, by order of state law or regulation, has a formal procedure for the evaluation of teachers. The system typically consists of one or two observations of teaching by a supervisor, who writes up his findings, provides feedback to the teacher, and completes an evaluation for insertion in the teacher's personnel file. Serious deficiencies may be addressed through the process and can lead, if procedures are carefully followed, to dismissal. That, however, is extremely rare.

The traditional approach to teacher evaluation is no longer adequate. One factor fueling the shift has been an expanded understanding of learning, and what constitutes good teaching. Another factor has been the promulgation, by professional organizations and many states and large school districts, of content standards for student learning. As these entities specify what students should know and be able to do, school districts have an obligation to ensure that their teachers be able to help students meet the higher standards. This interest in student learning has heightened interest, at all levels, in teacher performance.

The movement to adopt (or develop) content standards for student learning has its parallel in new approaches toward the evaluation of teaching. As educators learn more about teaching, in all its complexities, schools face the challenge of ensuring that all teachers are able to perform at those high levels (see box, "The Purposes of Evaluation"). In addition, a number of states have adopted teaching standards intended to guide local practitioners in the design of their evaluation systems. Although these standards are frequently stated too globally to translate directly into criteria for evaluation, they can provide a helpful context for local efforts.

Formative Versus Summative

It is clear that the list of purposes in the box can be divided into two broad categories: those purposes defined as *summative* (for the purpose of making consequential decisions) and those defined as *formative* (for the purpose of enhancing the professional skills of teachers). Screening out unsuitable candidates, dismissing incompetent teachers, and providing legally defensible evidence are all summative functions; providing constructive feedback, recognizing and reinforcing outstanding practice, providing direction for staff development, and unifying teachers and administrators around improved student learning are all formative. The two principal purposes of teacher evaluation, then, are (1) quality assurance and (2) professional development.

The Purposes of Evaluation

As Donald Haefele (1993) points out, a clear sense of purpose should govern the design of a teacher evaluation system. He identifies the following purposes that must be served, arguing that a system should

- screen out unqualified persons from certification and selection processes;
- provide constructive feedback to individual educators;
- recognize and help reinforce outstanding service;
- provide direction for staff development practices;
- provide evidence that will withstand professional and judicial scrutiny;
- aid institutions in terminating incompetent or unproductive personnel; and
- unify teachers and administrators in their collective efforts to educate students.

The relative importance of these two aspects of evaluation are significantly different for different groups of people. Legislators and policymakers tend to value the summative purposes, those of quality assurance and accountability. They make the point that public schools are, after all, public institutions, supported by taxpayer money, and that the public has a legitimate interest in the quality of the teaching that occurs there. It is through the system of teacher evaluation that members of the public, through their legislators, state officials, local boards of education, and administrators, ensure the quality of teaching. A parent, in other words, in entrusting the education of a child to the public schools, has a right to expect a certain minimum level of performance.

Educators, on the other hand, tend to think that teacher evaluation should be designed for the purpose of professional development and the improvement of teaching. Experienced practitioners argue that professional dialogue about teaching, in a safe environment, managed and led by teachers, is the only means by which teachers will improve their practice.

Serious Incompatibilities?

Not only do different individuals and groups disagree about the relative importance of the two main purposes of evaluation—quality assurance and professional growth—but some even argue that they are incompatible with one another. Some educators say that accountability requires a strict line of command, a fixed hierarchy. It must be evident to everyone where the buck stops, and whose job it is to do what. Evaluations are judgments; they are assessments of teaching, and they must be made as objectively as possible. They must also be made fairly, with no appearance of favoritism toward individuals based on friendship or bias grounded in irrelevant matters. Even if teachers organize and conduct the evaluations, as in peer review systems, the lines of responsibility and communication must be clear and unambiguous.

A concern for professional development, on the other hand, suggests a gentler, more trusting relationship between the teacher and the supervisor. In interactions focused on learning, the supervisor's role is more one of coach and mentor, rather than one of judge. The teacher does not have to hide concerns, but can voice them with an expectation of receiving assistance. When people perceive that an environment is conducive to professional learning, then they see it as profoundly different from one that yields objective evaluative judgments.

How to Resolve These Issues?

The possibility that the two essential purposes of teacher evaluation are incompatible is a serious indictment of current practice and is the result of several factors. In general, the culture surrounding teacher evaluation is not one of collegiality or professional inquiry; moreover, given the limitations of most systems, many educators regard teacher evaluation as an aspect of the profession of education that everyone must endure. To the extent that making judgments (the accountability function) requires clear evaluative criteria, the citing and weighing of evidence, and the neutralization of bias, evaluation appears inconsistent with the more supportive, nonjudgmental demeanor that most people associate with coaching (the professional development function).

Even more troubling, however, is the possibility that current evaluation practices achieve neither of their stated goals. Many teacher evaluation systems serve neither the accountability nor the professional development function. Certainly, Karen, in the Prologue, was unlikely to strengthen her teaching as a result of the evaluation process in which she was engaged. Similarly, Charles, even if he had serious concerns about Karen's performance, would have been unlikely to use the evaluation system to help her improve.

On close inspection, we can see that incompatibility between the two goals depends on the evaluation structures and procedures schools use. The principal argument of this book is that we can design evaluation systems in which educators can not only achieve the dual purposes of accountability and professional development, but can merge them. The following chapters show how.

2

The Once and Present Context for Teacher Evaluation: Important Lessons

In developing or redesigning local teacher evaluation systems, we must eventually answer two questions:

- What do we believe good teaching looks like?
- What are the processes and procedures that will best fit what we want our system to accomplish?

Neither question is new. Both have dominated the literature and the conversation about the evaluation of teaching and teachers since the beginning of the 20th century. As discussed in Chapter 1, teacher evaluation has had a checkered past. The good news is that over the past 30 years, educators and researchers have learned more about teaching and about how to effectively assess and enhance it. In this book, we address how a district's local teacher evaluation committee answers these questions and how it justifies its decisions; and we explore these questions in multifaceted ways and discuss many important lessons we have learned.

Shortcomings and Limiting Conditions

Chapter 1 discusses shortcomings that characterize traditional evaluation practices. Among them are (1) outdated, limited evaluative criteria and (2) the lack of shared values and assumptions about what constitutes good teaching. Both conditions create hurdles for local districts in the successful development of contemporary, effective teacher evaluation.

These shortcomings are often the result of two common conditions within local schools. First, school staff lack the time, training, and inclination to become knowledgeable about the best evidence emerging from the research on teaching. Second, despite this emerging evidence, school staff show a strong tendency "to pretend not to know what we know." It is easier to stick with what teachers have always done and believed, rather than go through the often painful process of changing current thinking about teaching—the way teachers practice it and the way people evaluate it.

The first of these conditions is legitimate. Because of the extraordinary demands on their

	FIGURE 2.1
	Historical Perspectives on the Research on Teaching
Decade	**Research on Teaching**
1950s	• Trait research
1960s	• Teacher effectiveness: the correlational years • Clinical supervision
1970s	• Hunter model • Learning styles
1980s	• Teacher effectiveness: the experimental period • Expectancy studies • Discipline models • Hunter derivatives • Effective schools research • Cooperative learning • Brain research
1990s	• Critical thinking • Content knowledge • Content pedagogy • Alternative assessment • Multiple intelligence • Collaborative learning • Cognitive learning theory • Constructivist classrooms • Authentic pedagogy • Engaged teaching and learning • Teaching for understanding
2000s	• Authentic pedagogy • Engaged teaching and learning • Teaching for understanding

time, teachers and administrators find it difficult to keep up with current research on teaching. Though keeping up is difficult, however, it is not impossible. Summaries of the research have been available for years and have had a strong, albeit not always positive, influence on teacher evaluation. Figure 2.1 provides a glimpse at the nature and focus of the research on teaching over the past 40 years. In several places in this book, we discuss the implications of this historical look at teaching and the impact on past and present evaluation systems.

A Short History of Research on Teaching

In the 1940s and 1950s, educators and researchers emphasized what are often called *presage variables*. These took the form of teacher traits (e.g., voice, appearance, emotional stability, trustworthiness, warmth, enthusiasm). Educators of this era believed that teachers who possessed these traits were more likely to perform effectively, so these traits became the centerpiece items in local teacher evaluation criteria. Unfortunately, with the exception of correlational data from the 1960s that suggested some connection between teacher enthusiasm and student achievement, no real evidence is available to link traits to good teaching or student learning.

The 1960s and 1970s brought a huge burst of energy to the teaching research and prompted a dramatic shift in the focus of teacher evaluation. The push to enhance basic skills acquisition and improve science and mathematics teaching encouraged research into what teachers did or could do to improve basic skills.

This time period coincided with significant advances in supervision skills and classroom-observation techniques. Researchers were developing "clinical supervision" as a way of enhancing instruction, and others were designing observation instruments that allowed more accurate depictions of what was occurring in classrooms. This ability to more accurately document teacher classroom behavior led to the design of studies seeking to identify what kinds of teacher behavior could be linked to student achievement. This *teacher effectiveness research*—or, as it was later named, the *research on teacher effects*—attempted and, in many cases, did show connections between teacher behavior or chunks of teacher behavior and basic skill acquisition. It was important work in that it began to form the basis for a set of fundamental teaching skills that are a part of the current framework for teaching.

The work of Madeline Hunter (e.g., 1982) and her colleagues at UCLA began at about this same time period. It was a theory-based way of looking at teaching that had its roots in a behavioristic view of basic learning theory. Extrapolating from such learning concepts as motivation, retention, and transfer, Hunter and her colleagues developed a set of prescriptive teaching practices designed to improve teacher decision making and thus enhance student learning. Through a powerful marketing program, the personal charisma and competence of Hunter, and a set of teaching strategies that reflected what many teachers felt they already did, the Hunter model dominated views of teaching into the 1980s and started a trend toward increased *instructionally focused* staff development that persists to this day.

As with the effects research, the Hunter model had its benefits—but no consistent evidence supported positive effects of the model on student learning. The effects research and the Hunter work encouraged an emphasis on *teacher-centered, structured classrooms*. Though designing such structured classrooms is an important part of a teacher's bag of tools, this is only a part of a larger range of skills and knowledge that comprises what is now viewed as effective teaching. To their credit, the majority of effects researchers—and Hunter herself—argued that their work should not be construed as a full-blown model for teaching. The ideas that emerged from the research and from common practice in the 1970s and 1980s helped expand our knowledge base.

The *downside* of the '70s and '80s was the way many state policymakers and local school districts interpreted and used these views of teaching. The development of state and local evaluation practices was often driven by evaluation criteria generated from lists of behaviors taken from the effects research or derived from Hunter's seven steps in lesson design (anticipatory set, statement of objective, instructional input, modeling, checking for understanding, guided practice, and independent practice). Developers of these evaluation instruments often provided rating scales and checklists to accompany evaluation criteria. These rating scales and checklists explicitly encouraged a single view of teaching. This was a clear misrepresentation of the research and promoted a simplistic, summative orientation toward evaluation that has persisted into the 1990s.

Despite the misrepresentation and misuse of the effects research, this approach made a significant contribution to education because it clearly confirmed the critical role that teachers play in student learning. It also provided education with a "knowledge base capable of moving the field beyond testimonials and unsupported claims toward scientific statements based on credible data" (Brophy, 1992, p. 5). At its best, the effects research provides the beginnings of a threshold that all teachers can be held up against.

A New View of Teaching and Learning

In the 1980s and 1990s, educators felt increased pressure to help students attain more complex outcomes. Concerns over the U.S. economy, projected changes in the skills and knowledge students would need to be successful in a changing job market, and a backlash to the perceived narrowness of the teacher effects research—all contributed to a noticeable shift in the study of teaching. The desired skills for students included such complex outcomes as critical thinking, problem solving, lifelong learning, collaborative learning, and deeper understanding. These outcomes, in turn, began to influence the language of teaching and what constitutes "good teaching."

These richer views of good teaching have resulted from shifts in our basic understanding of how children learn—from the behaviorist perspective to a view on learning derived from cognitive learning theory. This cognitive revolution and the research it generated has led to a greater understanding of the social nature of learning, the importance of context on understanding, the need for domain-specific knowledge in higher-order thinking, expert-novice differences in thinking and problem solving, and the belief that learners construct their own understanding of the topics they study (Eggen & Kauchak, 1996).

Adding also to the changing focus of teaching was a new understanding of content knowledge and how content is taught. Research on the interdependence of teaching methods and content has promoted new understanding about the dynamic interplay among content, teacher, learner, and context that must always be accommodated if teaching is to be effective. As educators and researchers better documented these expanded views of teaching and linked them to more complex student outcomes, they sought more reliable and valid forms of student assessment. The inseparable links among content instruction, appropriate assessment, and student learning have become more obvious. As a result of new technology that has supported more powerful statistical applications, current research has substantiated the power of these new skills and knowledge and has added to the growing picture of necessary teaching practices. In the simplest terms, the research supports fuller, richer pictures of teaching that use the "teacher effects" work as a foundation while going beyond it to focus on helping students acquire a *deep understanding* of the topics they study.

The research on effective teaching is available, and districts should take advantage of it. There is no reason for local districts not to borrow the work of others. Local committees should carefully review the language of externally developed standards to be sure that they represent what the district believes and can support. But there is an important lesson here. The past 40 years of research has produced an ever-evolving understanding of good teaching. If we plunge into denial ("pretending not to know what we know") or use other excuses ("been there, done that" or "what goes around, comes around"), we will miss out on knowledge accumulated through extensive reviews of best evidence and experience. Any district that is serious about developing new, effective evaluation and professional development programs must start with a rich set of teaching standards that reflect what we know. This lesson is at the heart of this book.

Conditions for Designing Effective Teacher Evaluation Systems

Evaluating teachers has been an educational activity since Socrates. Not until the 1960s, however, did any coherent focus on teacher appraisal begin to emerge. Since then it has become a much more serious and visible part of the study of schools. Researchers are conceiving of teacher evaluation as a mechanism for improving teaching and learning. As the research on teaching has made clear, schools are paying increased attention to the importance of the teacher to student learning—the issue of teacher quality.

The literature over the past 35 years has consistently supported two significant findings. First, teachers and administrators have always recognized the importance and necessity for evaluation; they have had serious misgivings, however, about how it was done and the lack of effect it had on teachers, their classrooms, and their students.

Second, evaluation systems designed to support teacher growth and development through an emphasis on formative evaluation techniques produced higher levels of satisfaction and more thoughtful and reflective practice while still being able to satisfy accountability demands.

This focus on using formative evaluation to support teacher growth and development is strongly supported by an emerging set of conditions that is shaping the context for the next generation of evaluation practices:

1. Reform and Restructuring Initiatives. A major part of school reform and restructuring involves the changing of the roles, responsibilities, and relationships between teachers and students and between teachers and administrators. Collaborative decision making, participatory management, team building, consensus strategies, and school improvement teams are all practices demanding that educators rethink traditional views of staff evaluation and staff development.

2. Increased Understanding of How Adults Grow, Develop, and Learn. Recent research and interest in adult development has produced a new set of insights into how to encourage continuing growth within mature teaching faculties. These insights point to the importance to adult professionals of their active involvement in instructional improvement efforts, of their working within a culture of collaboration, and of their access to positive reinforcement and support commensurate with their effort and productivity. These characteristics have not been a part of traditional evaluation practices.

3. Increased Awareness of the Importance and Complexity of Teaching. Current teaching research emphasizes the strong contextual nature of teaching, content pedagogy, authentic learning, engaged learning, collaborative learning, and teaching for more complex student outcomes. This research clearly supports teaching as a highly complex process that defies traditional methodology for assessing or assisting teachers. Richer forms of data collection and more self-reflection on the part of the teacher are necessary activities within the context of the new expectations for effective teaching.

4. Increased Focus on the Development of Teacher Expertise. Research in acknowledging and developing teacher expertise has provided increased understanding about both the natural and planned movement of teachers from the novice to the expert stage of development. The evidence clearly points to the need to differentiate both staff development and teacher evaluation to better fit the different pedagogical stages that characterize teaching staffs. This suggests the importance of building evaluation and staff development programs that allow and encourage this necessary differentiation.

5. New Understanding About Staff Development. In the past 10 years, researchers have contributed much new knowledge about the most effective forms of staff development for teachers. A set of guiding principles has emerged that is offering strong support for teacher evaluation programs that are directly linked to professional development. The most effective professional development programs are those that

- Stimulate and support site-based initiatives. Professional development is likely to have a greater effect on practice if it is closely linked to school initiatives to improve practice.
- Are grounded in knowledge about teaching. Good professional development should model constructivist teaching. Teachers need opportunities to explore, question, and debate to integrate new ideas into their repertoires and their classroom practice.
- Offer intellectual, social, and emotional engagement with ideas, materials, and colleagues. If teachers are to teach for deep understanding, they must be intellectually engaged in their disciplines and work regularly with others in their field.
- Demonstrate respect for teachers as professionals and as adult learners. Professional development should draw on the expertise of teachers and take differing degrees of teacher experience into account.
- Provide sufficient time and follow-up support for teachers to master new content and strategies and to integrate them into their practice.

6. The Reappraisal of Traditional Supervision Practices. In part as a result of the changing contextual factors discussed in Conditions 1–5, educators are questioning traditional forms of supervision. Two trends reflect the effect of changing contexts on supervision practices within evaluation systems. One is a move toward transforming the routine of classroom observation and follow-up. Sessions where administrators or peers help teachers reflect on their instruction are replacing administrator observations that are directed toward identifying strengths and weaknesses or areas for improvement. Even though the effect of traditional supervision practices has always been suspect, most experts agree that there is a benefit to being observed and then discussing and reflecting in some depth on what happened and why. A second trend is a move toward giving teachers options within supervision and evaluation systems. These options include such activities as participating in peer coaching, conducting action research projects, developing portfolios, and writing and carrying out self-directed professional development plans. Just as teachers have different teaching styles, so do they have different learning styles. New systems should allow for these differences.

Implications for Local Evaluation Committees

The trends and conditions provided here have important implications for local school districts engaged in designing new evaluation procedures. Using the conditions that have shaped the current context for teacher evaluation, schools can formulate the basic philosophy and principles that help them design new systems. Educators may wish to use the ideas presented in this chapter and in Chapters 3–7 to shape their philosophy.

Once educators have reached consensus on the general principles that will frame the system, the actual design can fall into place relatively quickly. There are two pieces of good news for local districts in regard to the options available for dealing with the question of "How can or should we do this?"

First, realistically there are not that many options from which to choose. The utility issue limits what is possible for most districts. By utility, we mean that there is only so much time and energy and only so many resources and levels of commitment that can be assumed in local districts for attending to teacher evaluation. Thus, local discussions should focus specifically on the following issues:

• Those practices that are realistic for the district in terms of teacher and administrator time demands.
• The availability of resources to support the training necessary to make new systems function effectively.
• The level of commitment that the administration, the board of education, and the teachers union have to break away from more traditional views of evaluation.

The second piece of good news is that many good examples are available to serve as models. Just as the accumulating evidence on teaching has provided a clearer picture of what constitutes good teaching, school districts throughout the United States have developed evaluation systems that reflect the best of what is known. Many of these exemplary systems have been in place long enough to have been evaluated for their effectiveness in meeting the stated purposes of the system, for promoting administrator and teacher satisfaction with the new procedures, for increasing the level and nature of professional learning occurring in the school, and for monitoring competent performance. Chapters 8–10 provide a look at some of the procedures and processes that comprise these model programs.

Lessons Learned About Teacher Evaluation

The processes that these "model" districts went through have produced some lessons and some directions that can be helpful to others. Some of these lessons are presented here and also incorporated into Chapters 3–6. Local educators should plan to engage stakeholders in conversations that attend to the following lessons we have learned.

1. New Evaluation Systems Should Be Directly Linked to the Mission of the School District

Educators need to see that building a new evaluation system is a major event. One of the fundamental conclusions of the school improvement research is that schools perform better when the parts all work together. School staffs should coordinate plans and activities that compose the basic workings of the school in a common effort to reach important school goals. Too often, evaluation systems have lacked any connection to other school initiatives. The adults who work in schools are the most important element in ensuring success for students. Linking selection of staff, the evaluation of the staff, and the professional development of the staff forms the basis for how schools and districts treat education professionals, support them, and value them. This issue and how the planned design will, in fact,

support, recognize, and involve the adult staff in meeting the stated mission of the school must be a part of the conversation. All recommended procedures and processes should be held up against the visible expression of what the district is trying to accomplish, especially in regard to student learning.

2. New Evaluation and Professional Development Systems Should Be Viewed as Continuing Processes

Traditionally, evaluation systems have emphasized short time lines for improvement activities (one-year goal setting experiences) and substantially unconnected assessment of performance every two, three, or four years. To fulfill the quality-assurance aspect of evaluation, evaluation of performance must be an ongoing process. Some type of formal activity may occur in different years, but that is only a part of the data collection that is constantly accumulating. Teachers and administrators interact on a continuing and daily basis. Information gained through the regular contact between staff—and also as a result of the natural physical proximity of relationships—are important and necessary parts of continuous appraisal. This should be made clear in the language of how the system operates ("All staff in the Addison School District are appraised continuously").

School staffs should set up alternative forms of evaluation that are directed at enhancing instruction through formative techniques and individual or team self-directed inquiry—also as continuous activities. Teachers and administrators should have the option of establishing professional development plans within the evaluation system over multiple years. If plans are to have any power to improve instruction, then staff must have the chance to spend the time needed to successfully carry out these more complex activities. But, once schools have implemented new alternative models, there should no longer be any downtime in the process. When staff reach some form of closure on a professional development plan, or some type of peer collaboration, or a self-directed inquiry activity, the staff members should establish a new plan. Growth and development are a process that must become part of the daily lives of professionals. There should be no time off from growing professionally.

3. New Evaluation Systems Should Emphasize Student Outcomes

In traditional teacher evaluation, educators have relied on the observation and judgment of teacher performance in the classroom. There has always been an undercurrent of interest and pressure to evaluate teachers on the achievement of their students. Chapter 5 discusses the difficulties of linking summative evaluation to student achievement, especially using norm-referenced standardized tests. These difficulties, however, should not prevent us from using student learning as a standard in evaluation systems. From the perspective of quality assurance, currently used standards for teaching performance, such as those in Danielson's 1996 book *Enhancing Professional Practice: A Framework for Teaching*, are much more valid descriptions of the variables linked to student learning than were available in the past.

In addition, the quality of the training available to supervisors and teachers in helping to identify, describe, and analyze classroom performance is significantly better than in the past. The issue of making summative judgments of teachers based on student achievement measures remains problematic; but school staffs can certainly learn from how well students perform, and incorporate that knowledge into the world of data obtained as they set up observations and hold conversations and conduct coaching sessions with teachers. In other words, we can work backwards from the data we get from student achievement.

The activities and events that educators develop as formative or alternative options within the professional development component of newly designed evaluation systems should focus on student learning. The new systems viewed as most effective require that the plans, the self-directed inquires, the collaborations among peers, or the collections of evidence of effort all be driven by a link to student learning goals and include measures of student learning. These are examples of the best form of linking performance to learning. Measures are used to enhance teaching and learning, not to judge it. A focus on student learning should pervade the language and attitude of newly designed systems.

4. There Must Be a Commitment to Allocating Adequate Resources to Allow New Systems to Be Successful

Many new evaluation systems have failed to achieve their desired outcomes, not because of faulty design or a lack of good intentions, but because schools and districts have not provided sufficient resources to support the plans. Schools need resources to support necessary training, to provide for planning time and released time for work on the professional development plans and activities generated by the options selected by staff, and to support the costs associated with gaining the knowledge and skills required to influence and shape teaching practices for producing the desired student outcomes. Communities and boards of education must realize that money spent to enhance and support teachers and supervisors in their work with students is an investment, not a cost. Local evaluation committees must determine and present the resource needs when they submit their recommendations to the board and to the union. As mentioned earlier, designing new evaluation and professional development systems is a major event. Improving student learning is not cheap.

The power of the new evaluation systems lies in their ability to focus attention on the importance of teaching and learning for students and teachers; to provide the means and the incentive for quality assurance, based on legitimate teaching standards; and to serve as the catalyst for encouraging and supporting professional learning through focused, collaborative activities. The conditions and the knowledge that have shaped the present context for evaluation should provide any local district with the justification to support breaking away from traditional evaluation practices and to stop pretending not to know that we do know what good teaching should look like and how we can enhance and support it.

3

A Blueprint for Teacher Evaluation

Some educators equate teacher evaluation with classroom observation; others equate it with the forms used. Revising their system of evaluation, then, becomes a matter of changing the forms, or the forms used in an observation. Although evaluation forms are important in defining the structure of an evaluation process and the types of professional conversation surrounding it, forms do not constitute the system. An effective teacher evaluation system is far more complex than the forms and must contain three essential elements:

• A coherent definition of the domain of teaching (the "What?"), including decisions concerning the standard for acceptable performance ("How good is good enough?").
• Techniques and procedures for assessing all aspects of teaching (the "How?").
• Trained evaluators who can make consistent judgments about performance, based on evidence of the teaching as manifested in the procedures.

In addition, in designing (or revising) its system of evaluation, a school district should follow a process that includes many perspectives—those of teachers, administrators, and the leadership of the teacher's association.

The challenge confronting designers of an evaluation system is to (1) encourage professional learning and, at the same time, (2) ensure the quality of teaching. Thanks to recent experience with assessments, such as those developed by the National Board for Professional Teaching Standards, educators are now in a good position to address this design challenge.

In this chapter, we explore the three essential elements of a coherent evaluation system, as mentioned previously. We then outline the demands of quality assurance and the requirements of an environment for professional learning—and describe the means by which schools and districts may merge the two aspects into a single system.

The Nature of Quality Assurance

The requirements for quality assurance link directly to the structure described here for the elements of an evaluation system (the "what," the "how," and trained evaluators).

The "What"

Central to the notion of quality assurance in teaching is a clear and coherent definition of exemplary practice (for more information, see

Chapter 4). Some states have articulated standards of practice (e.g., the California Standards for the Teaching Profession, the Texas Learner-Centered Proficiencies, and Vermont's *Standards for Vermont Educators*), and districts are required to use these as the basis of their evaluation procedures. Other districts have found the components of professional practice described in *Enhancing Professional Practice: A Framework for Teaching* (Danielson, 1996) useful as a structure for evaluation. Figure 3.1 lists the four domains and 22 components of this structure.

As part of defining good teaching, we need to establish the relative importance of the different criteria ("Are they all equally important?"); the levels of performance ("What does it look like when it is done well?"); and a standard for acceptable, or exemplary, performance ("How good is good enough, and how good is very good?"). The standards of performance must be clear and unambiguous, and both publicly known and publicly derived (see Chapter 4 for a full discussion of these issues).

To ensure teaching quality, schools and districts must base the evaluative criteria on recent research on teaching and learning. This ensures the validity of the criteria. In addition, the criteria should include all the important aspects of teaching and not be limited to only a part of what teachers do. For example, an evaluation system that defines teaching solely in terms of what teachers do in their classroom interactions with students misses all the important aspects of the teaching role that occur outside that venue. And yet, who could argue that communication with families is not an important part of a teacher's role, and should not therefore be part of an evaluation system?

The "How"

To ensure a valid evaluation system, when schools and districts identify certain criteria as contributing to good practice, they should ensure that teachers will be able to demonstrate the criteria. If, for example, communicating with families is one of the evaluative criteria, how will teachers demonstrate their skill? Because this skill is not visible in a classroom observation, schools and districts must devise other procedures to evaluate it.

Evaluation processes must allow for evaluators to make reasonable judgments regarding the quality of teaching; and schools and districts must include procedures to offer intensive assistance, if needed, to teachers who are struggling to perform adequately. And, if performance is not at least minimally acceptable, after schools and districts have provided assistance and have followed all the requirements of due process, schools must devise manageable procedures for termination.

The "how" of teacher evaluation includes many items, ranging from the general procedures (possibly differentiated for novices and experienced teachers), the time lines, the personnel involved, and the specific forms and procedures used. All these should be clear to everyone involved and implemented in an equitable manner (see Chapters 5 and 6 for more information about procedural matters).

Trained Evaluators

Those making evaluative judgments must be adequately trained so their judgments are accurate, consistent, and based on evidence. From the standpoint of those being evaluated (teachers), it must not matter who is conducting the evaluation; the result should be the same

---

FIGURE 3.1
Components of Professional Practice

Domain 1: Planning and Preparation

Domain 1 (Planning and Preparation) includes comprehensive understanding of the content to be taught, knowledge of the students' backgrounds, and designing instruction and assessment. Its components are:

1a. Demonstrating knowledge of content and pedagogy

1b. Demonstrating knowledge of students

1c. Selecting instructional goals

1d. Demonstrating knowledge of resources

1e. Designing coherent instruction

1f. Assessing student learning

Domain 2: The Classroom Environment

Domain 2 (The Classroom Environment) addresses the teacher's skill in establishing an environment conducive to learning, including both the physical and interpersonal aspects of the environment. Its components are:

2a. Creating an environment of respect and rapport

2b. Establishing a culture for learning

2c. Managing classroom procedures

2d. Managing student behavior

2e. Organizing physical space

Domain 3: Instruction

Domain 3 (Instruction) is concerned with the teacher's skill in engaging students in learning the content, and includes the wide range of instructional strategies that enable students to learn. Its components are:

3a. Communicating clearly and accurately

3b. Using questioning and discussion techniques

3c. Engaging students in learning

3d. Providing feedback to students

3e. Demonstrating flexibility and responsiveness

Domain 4: Professional Responsibilities

Domain 4 (Professional Responsibilities) addresses a teacher's additional professional responsibilities, including self-assessment and reflection, communication with parents, participating in ongoing professional development, and contributing to the school and district environment. Its components are:

4a. Reflecting on teaching

4b. Maintaining accurate records

4c. Communicating with families

4d. Contributing to the school and district

4e. Growing and developing professionally

4f. Showing professionalism

Source: Danielson, C. (1996). *Enhancing professional practice: A framework for teaching.* Alexandria, VA: Association for Supervision and Curriculum Development.

---

regardless of the identity of the evaluator. This consistency of judgment on the part of trained evaluators is an essential guarantee of the reliability of the system as a whole.

The training of evaluators has several important dimensions:

• First, evaluators must be able to recognize examples of the evaluative criteria in action. Classroom events and instructional artifacts constitute mere data; which data should evaluators select as evidence of the different evaluative criteria? The evidence selected should not only be relevant to the various criteria, but it should also be representative; not only negative evidence, for example, should be identified.

• Second, evaluators must interpret the evidence for some aspect of teaching against the evaluative criteria. As any careful observer of teaching recognizes, there is more than one possible interpretation of an event; correct interpretation is an important aspect of professional judgment about teaching.

• Last, the evaluator must make a judgment about the teacher's performance, linking the interpretations to the descriptions of levels of performance. In addition, evaluators must be able to hold reflective conversations and provide constructive feedback.

Is any of this consistent with professional learning? At first glance, it is difficult to see how, because the demands of quality assurance sound rigid and unlikely to promote professional growth. But before we conclude that they are incompatible, we should take a closer look at the nature of professional learning.

The Nature of Professional Learning

Several factors contribute to professional learning, including reflection on practice, collaboration, and self-assessment.*

Reflection on Practice

Few activities are more powerful for professional learning than reflection on practice. As

Schon (1983) has pointed out, we learn not so much from our experience, but from our reflection *on* our experience. Reflection requires asking (and answering) such questions as "Were those reasonable learning expectations for my students?" "Would different groupings have worked better?" and "How do I know the students have really learned this concept?"

Many experienced teachers spontaneously engage in such reflection on at least an informal basis. But few novice teachers do so, and many experienced teachers rarely devote the time to it that sustained reflection (and therefore real learning) requires.

Schools and districts may include reflection on practice at many points in a teacher evaluation process. Self-assessment, descriptions and commentaries about learning activities, and analysis of student work all depend on thoughtful consideration of what the teacher intended and whether she achieved her goals.

Collaboration

Some educators are able to engage in reflection on practice on their own and will devote considerable time to the endeavor. Most people, however, find it difficult to attain the self-discipline required for such inquiry; and it tends to be crowded out by more immediately pressing concerns. Thus, a system that builds in collaboration, particularly if that collaboration demands reflection on practice, is more likely to yield genuine effort than one that does not.

The isolation of teachers has been well documented. On their evaluation forms after a workshop, many teachers will write that the opportunity to discuss issues with their colleagues was the most beneficial aspect of the day. Teaching is highly complex, and most teachers have scant opportunity to explore

---

*The characteristics of an environment for professional growth presented here owe a debt to the discussion by Lee Schulman (1997).

common problems and possible solutions, or share new pedagogical approaches with their colleagues. As educators design systems for evaluation, they can include provision for professional conversation—among teachers and between teachers and administrators.

Collaboration offers another real benefit—the provision of alternative points of view. Most educators find that a colleague's perspective on a situation is a little different from their own, and that this different view offers possibilities that theirs alone does not. Teachers find it difficult to sustain an interpretation of an event in the face of conflicting evidence from a colleague. Thus, collaboration offers the possibility of a more balanced, and more accurate, interpretation of practice.

Self-Assessment and Self-Directed Inquiry

Teachers are professionals; they are practitioners of a complex craft. Teachers tend to know where their areas of strength and relative weakness lie and are keen to bring all areas of their practice to higher levels. If provided with a safe and respectful environment, most teachers will choose to concentrate their efforts at professional growth in those areas in which they have the greatest need.

The principles of adult learning show that when people use self-assessment and self-directed inquiry in professional development, they are more likely to sustain their learning, in more disciplined ways, than when outsiders impose professional development requirements. When people select their own "problem" to be solved, their own project to pursue, they devote greater energy to it than if someone else has chosen the issue.

The basis for the selection of areas of practice to work on is, or should be, self-assessment,

possibly supplemented by evaluator input. Experienced teachers are typically able to assess their own practice accurately, whereas novices, depending on their preparation programs, may be less skilled in this activity. Evaluation systems, then, should include opportunities for self-assessment and self-directed professional growth for experienced teachers, and guided self-assessment for novices. Of course, if an administrator has reason to believe that a teacher's self-assessment is not fully accurate, if the teacher is unaware of aspects of practice that need attention, those should be noted and added to the areas deserving of attention. But the teacher's self-assessment should always be the starting point for the discussion.

A Community of Learners

When teachers collaborate on a project to advance their knowledge, they create, for themselves, a community of learners. They are, and feel themselves to be, a small group in pursuit of common learning. There is no difference in status—all individuals are of equal rank—and all are engaged in activities to advance their understanding. In addition, the environment must be safe for risk-taking; fear can play no role in a community of learners.

To derive the full benefits of collaborative inquiry, schools and districts need to put forth a systematic effort. A culture of professional inquiry does not happen by itself; schools must create it. This culture can take many forms—for example, protected time for study groups to meet, substitute teachers to cover classes during observations, or funds to enable teachers to attend professional meetings or to acquire professional materials. Alternatively, a school can institute a system of "critical friends" through which teachers meet together to offer constructive suggestions to one another. Through such activities, and the tangible support for them, a school or district demonstrates its commitment to the continuing professional growth of its teachers.

This commitment is also reflected in the more intangible nature of the culture of the school. In a school in which people value professional inquiry, the school's leadership does not tolerate negative comments about students in the faculty lounge, nor put-downs directed against fellow teachers. Teachers demonstrate their willingness to share materials they have developed and to collaborate on the challenges presented by students who are having difficulty in their learning. In such a school, teachers do not work in isolation: Their doors are open and they freely exchange perspectives on their teaching strategies. Procedures for teacher evaluation should include activities contributing to a culture for professional inquiry and ways to support such activities.

The Role of Formative Assessment

Learning almost always involves formative assessment; indeed, it is so embedded in the process of teaching and learning that it is easy to overlook. Consider the process of learning to play golf. A novice would need to find a good teacher, one who could offer instruction and help the learner improve her skill. This coach, of course, would be a good golfer; he would be skilled at the different aspects of the game. In addition, however, the coach would be a skilled diagnostician; offering encouragement is not enough. It would not be sufficient for the coach to observe a swing and to say: "That was good; try again." Instead, the coach would offer specific advice, based on a clear diagnosis: "You are dropping your right shoulder," or "You are

turning your hips too far to the left," or "You are looking up before you swing." That is, the coach has *assessed* the novice's practice, and is offering feedback, for the purpose of advancing her learning. The coach is not judging her, but is assessing her performance.

This distinction is critical and can help us design powerful evaluation systems that promote professional learning. For example, a teaching coach might observe a class and note the type of questions the teacher asked. If they were primarily low-level, with a single correct answer, this information would be of value to the teacher, and could be used to improve practice.

Reflecting the Requirements for Professional Learning in the "Blueprint"

Just as the requirements for quality assurance can be reflected in the elements of the "blueprint," so can those of an environment (the "what") for professional learning.

The "What"

The definition of exemplary practice—with its levels of performance and, especially, the process used to derive that definition—can advance the principles of professional learning. When educators consider what is good teaching, and how it is manifested in a variety of settings; when they debate the levels of performance, and whether these apply equally in all contexts, they engage in professional conversation, in a collaborative setting; and they usually also reflect on their own practice.

The environment for such conversations, of course, must be safe for taking professional risks. As teachers consider drafts of an evaluation document and debate whether all the evaluative criteria are valid in all contexts, or whether the descriptions of levels of performance apply in their setting, they must be free to speak their minds without fear of negative consequences. The discussions must be genuine professional conversations, without undercurrents of point-scoring, or posturing, that occasionally characterize such debates.

These conversations invariably engage teachers in self-assessment and reflection; it is virtually impossible for a practitioner to consider descriptions of levels of performance of a skill of teaching without privately asking questions such as "How do I do that?" or "At what level am I performing on this standard?" In addition, as teachers consider the wording of different components of teaching and their elements and compare their impressions and practices with one another, they trade techniques and learn new strategies from their colleagues. These conversations are rich—focused on the quality of teaching and contributing much to the professional learning of those participating.

The "How"

Of all the various elements of a system for teacher evaluation that contribute to professional learning, the procedures used contribute the most. The experience of candidates for advanced certification by the National Board for Professional Teaching Standards is instructive in this regard: Virtually everyone who goes through the process, *even those who are not successful,* report that they have become better teachers because of the effort.

This phenomenon then becomes a design question: "How can we design systems for teacher evaluation that result in professional learning? What can we ask teachers to do, as part of the process, that is professionally rewarding and growth-producing?" Schools and districts may ask teachers, as part of their evaluation process, to submit a unit of study from their class, an activity from that unit, and some samples of student work from the activity—and write a brief commentary about the activity and the student work. If evaluators ask teachers questions that demand reflection and thoughtfulness, and if teachers must select student work that provides evidence of student achievement, teachers are almost guaranteed to learn from the process. If they must answer questions such as "How does this activity deepen student understanding of the concept?" or "What do these student work samples tell me about their level of understanding?" they are required to reflect on the activity, and the experience of individual students with it. In asking teachers to submit this unit, activity, and student work, the evaluation system is not imposing extra "work": Teachers design such activities and collect student work on a daily basis. In other words, the activity represents, as Mari Pearlman (personal communication, 1994) of the Educational Testing Service has called it, a "natural harvest" of their work. Granted, teachers don't always reflect systematically on students' work or analyze an activity and the larger unit in light of it, and they certainly don't write a brief commentary about their reflections. Being asked to do so once a year, however, is not an unreasonable request, and such reflection can contribute to the development of valuable habits of mind.

The challenge, then, for designers of evaluation systems is to structure the evaluation procedures so that teachers are required to do certain things, the very doing of which promotes professional learning. These required activities can certainly include an administrator's observation of classroom teaching. But the evaluation system can also include self-assessment and conversation about the appropriate placement on charts describing levels of performance. The system can ask teachers to provide concrete evidence of student learning. The evaluation system can also ask teachers to provide samples of nonclassroom responsibilities (such as parent communication; maintenance of accurate records; or contributions to school and district projects, such as participation on committees). If evaluation systems are well designed, teachers take an active role in the process and learn from their participation.

Trained Evaluators

The procedures used to orient teachers and to train evaluators in the use of the evaluation system can also represent valuable professional work. When educators discuss the evaluative criteria, when they examine evidence of teaching (such as tapes or commentaries) and determine, together, the level of performance represented, they are engaging in valuable professional dialogue. And the consensus derived through such dialogue serves the district well in forging a common understanding of what good teaching actually looks like.

Merging Quality Assurance and Professional Learning

So how can schools and districts integrate the demands of quality assurance and professional learning into a single system? What characteristics of an evaluation system satisfy the requirements of both, taking into account the dysfunctional aspects of most current approaches? The principal features of such an integrated system include a differentiated approach, a culture of professional inquiry, and carefully designed evaluation activities.

Differentiation

A teacher's career, like that of other professionals, has a distinct life cycle. The job is complex, and skillful practice requires considerable time and support to acquire. But once a teacher attains a certain level of proficiency, professional learning takes a different form from that experienced earlier in the process, and can be more self-directed. And if teachers slip in their skill, if their performance drops below a certain acceptable level, they can also benefit from higher levels of support and more intensive assistance. This suggests that the procedures used in the evaluation process can be different for those at different stages in their careers.

Thus, schools and districts should differentiate their evaluation system for teachers, according to their professional needs. Many schools have designed systems with three "tracks": separate activities and time lines for *novice* (or probationary, or nontenured) teachers, for *experienced* (or career, or tenured) teachers, and for those *needing intensive assistance* or a plan of action (experienced teachers for whom the next step is dismissal for inadequacy in teaching). (See Chapters 8–10 for more information on these three tracks.)

A Culture of Professional Learning

An environment for learning, whether learning by students or by adults, does not occur spontaneously; it must be planned and honored in practice. While largely under the leadership of administrators, all educators play a role in establishing and maintaining this environment. Its elements include the following:

- A *Collaborative Culture of Professional Inquiry*. There are no experts in the complex act of teaching, and all practitioners can learn from one another. A collaborative culture of inquiry requires that teachers and administrators all expect the activities they do as part of the evaluation process to be professionally rewarding. Leadership is required to maintain focus on the quality of student learning, but within that context everyone in the school is "in it together" to enhance student achievement, and their efforts should be seen as working in concert.

- *(For Novice Teachers) A Spirit of Support and Assistance*. A spirit of support and assistance is best institutionalized through a mentoring or induction program. But even in the absence of a formalized structure, its spirit can prevail, and would eliminate such outrageous practices as assigning new teachers the most difficult students, or the most preparations, or the one assignment without a permanent classroom, etc. Such professional "hazing" (Linda Darling-Hammond's term for it) is inexcusable, results in unnecessary stress, and is partly responsible for high rates of attrition and premature cynicism among new teachers.

In an effective evaluation system, such a spirit of support is reflected in the willingness of experienced teachers to invite their novice colleagues into their classrooms to observe, to discuss strategies with them after school, and to help them prepare for the events of the evaluation process. New teachers should not feel that they are alone in their professional life.

- *(For Tenured Teachers) Two Presumptions: Of Competence and Continued Professional Growth*. Once teachers have achieved career (or tenured) status, they are full members of a professional community and should be treated as such. One manifestation of that status is the explicit acceptance of the two presumptions of competence and of continuing professional growth. The first presumption, that of competence, states that unless notified to the contrary, the teacher's performance is at least at a satisfactory level. It conveys the notion that the job (and therefore the livelihood) of a teacher is never in question. This presumption alone can remove some of the anxiety from the evaluation process, and contribute to an environment safe for taking risks.

But the presumption of competence is, by itself, insufficient; it must be accompanied by the presumption of continuing professional learning. This second presumption states that it is every teacher's responsibility to continue to grow professionally, and that teachers may stagnate in their professional knowledge. Both presumptions must be present; the first without the latter breeds complacency; the second without the first undermines trust.

Within the context of an evaluation system, these presumptions play out both in the required activities of the process and the manner in which they are done. The activities, particularly if a school adopts some aspect of the self-directed professional growth phase as part of the evaluation of career professionals, must be recognized as opportunities for learning. In completing them, all teachers expect to improve their practice. But in addition, the presumption of competence suggests that the evaluation process is simply an opportunity to improve one's craft still further.

These two presumptions, together with a culture of inquiry, produce an environment safe for professional risk-taking. Teachers know that, even during a formal, evaluation observation, they can try a new strategy and receive feedback on it, or they could submit, as part of their portfolio, an instructional artifact and student work they wanted to discuss with a more senior colleague. It would not have to be a "showcase" effort, but one in the course of development.

Activities as Part of the Evaluation Process, the Doing of Which Contribute to Professional Learning

Sound measurement requires that all the aspects of the domain of teaching be capable of being assessed through the evaluation process. But there are design decisions to be made: some activities yield far more professional learning than do others.

By requiring self-assessment, working in teams on a focus area, and reflecting on one's practice through portfolio exercises, an evaluation system can promote professional learning in teachers. No matter how skilled a person embarking on any of those activities, the activities themselves guide and support growth. Even with no evaluation system, if teachers simply did those things, their practice would improve. By making them part of the evaluation system, however, the school district ensures that they will occur.

Some newly developed evaluation systems require that teachers conduct a self-assessment, establish professional growth goals, and participate in a study group with colleagues to pursue a topic of common interest. (Such a requirement engages the teachers in self-assessment, reflection on practice, self-directed inquiry, collaboration, and professional conversation.) Then, in addition to classroom observations, teachers are asked to submit evidence of their professional skill, in the form of planning documents, samples of student work (with a

---

FIGURE 3.2
Merging Quality Assurance and Professional Learning in Teacher Evaluation

Item/Procedure	Quality Assurance	Professional Learning
Definition of Teaching, including levels of performance	• Clear, unambiguous • Research based • Locally validated	Process of development results in shared understanding
Techniques and Procedures for Evaluation	• Sources of information document all evaluative criteria • Evaluators follow procedures, including due process • Procedures are equitable	Designed to maximize professional learning and reflection on practice
Training for Evaluators and Teachers	• Evaluators make consistent judgments based on evidence • Interrater agreement	The process of training itself builds consensus and develops shared understanding

commentary), and other evidence of their professionalism (such as parent communication, contributions to the school and district, etc). Assembling and selecting these documents require deep reflection on practice; describing them to an administrator engages a teacher in professional conversation.

Although the demands of quality assurance and professional learning seem, at first, to be incompatible, they are, in fact, complementary. Careful design work is needed, to be sure. But the concepts themselves can co-exist, and even strengthen one another (for a summary, see Figure 3.2).

4

The Evaluative Criteria, or the "What"

The cornerstone of any evaluation system is the set of evaluative criteria on which a school or district bases its teacher evaluations. How should we judge a teacher's performance? Determining the criteria is not the same thing as developing an evaluation system; however, no evaluation system is complete without a set of clear, unambiguous criteria that, taken together, define good teaching.

What, then, constitutes excellence (or adequacy) in teaching? By what criteria do we define superior teaching? When a teacher earns a reputation in a community for being a wonderful educator, when administrators receive more requests for placement into that teacher's classes than they can handle, when a teacher is highly respected by colleagues—on what basis do people make such judgments? Do students in those classes have a lot of fun? Do they participate in exciting activities? Do they normally do extremely well on the state assessment?

Alternatively, when a teacher acquires a reputation, among both students and parents, for poor teaching, on what is that reputation based? It might reflect inconsistent or unfair grading standards, or the display of favoritism in classroom interactions. It might be a consequence of unclear explanations of concepts or procedures, so students don't have a good understanding of the content. Or, the reputation might develop over many years, if the students of a particular teacher consistently do poorly on a state's assessment. Clearly, when students, parents, and administrators make judgments about teaching, they base their assessment on evidence of performance. These judgments may be informal, but they are judgments nonetheless.

Inputs or Outputs?

Standards of teaching state what teachers should know and be able to do in the exercise of their profession. People express this concept in one of two fundamental ways: in terms of what teachers do, or in terms of the results they achieve. The former could be called "inputs"—an enumeration of teacher tasks reflecting all the complexity of the work. (These lists of tasks need not be checklists of specific types of behavior, but they identify all the different aspects of teaching that yield high levels of student learning.) The latter, on the other hand, can be considered "outputs"—the results teachers achieve in their work, for example in the extent of student learning or performance, as an indication of the quality of teaching.

Of these two approaches, the former has the longer history of use in the evaluation of teaching. More recently, however, in response to greater calls for accountability of teachers and whole schools, many districts (some as required by their state legislatures or boards of education) are incorporating measures of student learning into the definition of teaching to be used in evaluation.

This chapter considers both inputs and outputs and points out the strengths and limitations of each approach to teacher evaluation.

"Inputs," or What Teachers Do

In the "input" tradition, the definition of good teaching—the set of evaluative criteria—refers to what teachers do in the course of their professional practice, the tasks that fill their days (and frequently their evenings). Over the past 20 years, the definition of good teaching has gradually changed, from approaches that specified actual teaching behaviors to those that relied more heavily on methods that promote student conceptual understanding.

Some states have incorporated criteria for teaching in their licensing procedures. Georgia led the way (in 1980) with the Teacher Performance Assessment Instrument (TPAI), followed by North Carolina, Florida, Connecticut, and other states. Effective teaching, as described by Madeline Hunter (1982) and other researchers, is an example of this tradition that won widespread national attention during the 1980s.

The Educational Testing Service (ETS) drew on these efforts in the development of Praxis III: Classroom Performance Assessments for Licensing Beginning Teachers. The development process incorporated extensive literature reviews, expert panels, job analyses, and pilot and field-testing. More recently, ASCD's book *Enhancing Professional Practice: A Framework for Teaching* (Danielson, 1996) was based on the Praxis III research and linked to the principles of exemplary practice described by the Interstate New Teacher Assessment and Support Consortium (INTASC). (The components of this framework appear as Figure 3.1 in Chapter 3 of this book.) The book expands the teaching skills identified in Praxis III to include the work of experienced teachers, and the book reflects the vision of teaching and learning embedded in the work of the National Board for Professional Teaching Standards (NBPTS). This framework, building on the earlier work of others, is the latest effort along these lines; and many school districts have used it as an organizing structure in defining effective teaching and establishing criteria for their evaluation systems.

Issues Raised by the "Inputs" Model

Local developers of teacher evaluation systems face many complexities in defining effective teaching practices. The issues to consider include important assumptions, teacher acceptance of the criteria, and the level of detail.

Assumptions. Any list of teaching skills (and its accompanying descriptions of levels of performance) reflects assumptions regarding teaching and learning and, indeed, of what is worth learning and how it should be learned. Both of these have been gradually changing. Some earlier efforts to define effective teaching reflected a rather mechanical, "information-transmission" view of teaching. Although the acquisition of information is, and always will be, an important goal of education, an exclusive focus on it is increasingly incompatible with current theories of learning and inappropriate to the types of learning embodied in most content standards that states and professional organizations have developed.

The list of teaching skills, in other words, must reflect current best knowledge about learning and what students must learn. For example, the National Council of Teachers of Mathematics (NCTM) standards emphasize problem-solving in mathematics, a skill that cannot be learned through rote memorization. Therefore, a school attempting to implement those standards must define teaching in ways that incorporate instructional approaches likely to improve students' skills in problem solving.

To take another look at this example: Suppose your school or district does not accept the NCTM standards. Then the criteria for defining good teaching for your school might not emphasize the cognitive research that underlies the NCTM standards—or might interpret it differently. Thus, no matter what position your school or district takes on standards or educational research findings, it is important to recognize the theoretical underpinnings of any description of teaching, and to know the assumptions about content and learning theory on which it is based.

Acceptance. An important acid test of any list of teaching skills is that it be acceptable to the teachers affected by it, that it reflect what practitioners know of their work. Therefore, schools and districts developing a definition of teaching need to provide opportunities for wide discussion and customization. This process can both validate the criteria and develop ownership and commitment. When

such discussion involves a wide range of teachers and administrators, it will yield a document that people will accept enthusiastically.

When teachers join the staff of a school with a set of evaluative criteria already in place, they do not have the opportunity to contribute to the development of the criteria. If they know that the voices of their colleagues were heard in the process, however, and if they know they will be able to offer their ideas when the system is next revised, they can be assured that the administration did not arbitrarily select the evaluative criteria.

Levels of Specificity. Educators may compose lists of teaching skills at various levels of generality or specificity. For example, INTASC identified 10 principles and 53 performance indicators. The NBPTS identified 5 key principles, which are then further elaborated in the standards for each of the levels and disciplines for which assessments have been developed. California's Standards for the Teaching Profession are organized into six standards, with 32 elements. ETS's Praxis III is built around four domains and 19 criteria; Danielson's (1996) *Enhancing Professional Practice: A Framework for Teaching* organizes teaching into four domains and 22 components.

The list of teaching skills should be sufficiently detailed to encourage specific conversations about practice, and yet not so elaborate that people cannot keep it in mind. For example, at one time Louisiana's standards for the evaluation of teaching included 145 separate criteria; though the approach had great merit, it included too many criteria for most people to use easily.

Redundancy. A list of teaching skills that forms the basis of an evaluation system should avoid redundancy. That is, the list should include each of the important aspects of teaching only once. Admittedly, teaching is highly complex, with skills that overlap and intertwine; but it is possible to identify discrete aspects of it. Where possible, the different tasks of teaching should be separate from one another.

Feedback Options. Specific evaluative criteria enable mentors, coaches, and supervisors to provide feedback on specific aspects of teaching and should enable teachers to set goals for improving their practice. Some lists of teaching skills define teaching rather globally, with the different standards taking a different perspective in describing what is a holistic effort. Although such lists reinforce the connections between the different aspects of teaching, they are less useful for conducting assessments and providing feedback on specific aspects of teaching.

Levels of Performance. A set of teaching skills to define teaching is incomplete unless it includes a description of differing levels of performance. These descriptions serve to define the points on the rating scale in operational terms. If, for example, an evaluation system identifies three points on a scale of performance (such as "needs improvement," "satisfactory," and "outstanding"), what do those terms actually mean for each of the criteria? What specific events in a classroom would cause a teacher's performance on, for example, "managing classroom procedures" to be judged "unsatisfactory"?

Figure 4.1 (p. 36) is an example of levels of performance (from Danielson's 1996 *Enhancing Professional Practice: A Framework for Teaching*). Charts like this one have helped schools and districts around the United States revise their teacher evaluation systems. Both teachers and supervisors find the descriptions of levels of performance helpful because the descriptions

focus on teaching practice and note what changes would have to be made to qualify for the next level.

The levels of performance permit the discussion about teaching to be nonpersonal; that is, if an evaluator cites events from a classroom observation as evidence for a certain placement on the levels of performance, the language serves to mediate the conversation. And if the teacher disagrees with the judgment, he can offer different evidence that might yield a different judgment. With the levels of performance chart on a table between them, a teacher is less likely to consider a supervisor's judgment a personal attack; rather, it is judgment, using clear criteria, based on evidence.

In the debates regarding exactly how they should describe the levels of performance, educators in a school or district develop a common understanding of the evaluative criteria themselves and—through the examples of practice they generate—engage in important professional conversation. Some of the descriptions of levels of performance, however, may not apply in the same way in all settings. For example, the degree to which a teacher knows her students (their individual interests, their cultural heritage, and their preparation in the subject) is almost certainly different for a kindergarten teacher with 18 students than for a high school band teacher with 300. (This is not to suggest that a high school band teacher should not know her students and their level of skill on their instruments. But the sheer numbers involved make it difficult for teachers to have the level of knowledge of individual students that teachers with fewer students would be expected to display.)

There is another reason to be flexible in applying the levels of performance to the

FIGURE 4.1
Domain 2: The Classroom Environment

Component 2a: Creating an Environment of Respect and Rapport

Level of Performance

Element	Unsatisfactory	Basic	Proficient	Distinguished
Teacher Interaction with Students	Teacher interaction with at least some students is negative, demeaning, sarcastic, or inappropriate to the age or culture of the students. Students exhibit disrespect for teacher.	Teacher-student interactions are generally appropriate but may reflect occasional inconsistencies, favoritism, or disregard for students' cultures. Students exhibit only minimal respect for teacher.	Teacher-student interactions are friendly and demonstrate general warmth, caring, and respect. Such interactions are appropriate to developmental and cultural norms. Students exhibit respect for teacher.	Teacher demonstrates genuine caring and respect for individual students. Students exhibit respect for teacher as an individual, beyond that for the role.
Student Interaction	Student interactions are characterized by conflict, sarcasm, or put-downs.	Students do not demonstrate negative behavior toward one another.	Student interactions are generally polite and respectful.	Students demonstrate genuine caring for one another as individuals and as students.

Source: Danielson, C. (1996). *Enhancing professional practice: A framework for teaching.* Alexandria, VA: Association for Supervision and Curriculum Development (p. 80).

evaluation of teaching: Variation of performance is to be expected, because of many factors. For example, most teachers will demonstrate higher levels of performance in January than in October—once they have come to know their students and have established their classroom routines. Similarly, the longer a teacher has taught at a certain grade level, and in a single school or district (as the teacher becomes familiar with the curriculum and with the culture of the school and the district), the higher will be that teacher's level of performance. We

should regard the levels of performance, therefore, as levels of performance of *teaching*, not of *teachers*, and look at judgments of performance in that light.

If, for example, a teacher has taught 5th grade for 10 years, he will have developed many techniques and strategies suitable for that setting. If, however, he is reassigned to 2nd grade, he will have to adapt many of those strategies and learn some new skills. Second graders are different from 5th graders, and certainly the curriculum is different. Similarly, a teacher who has been teaching in a certain school for several years may discover that she will need different techniques if she is reassigned to another school across town. Finally, a high school science teacher who has focused on biology for several years will probably have to devote considerable planning time to a new section of chemistry. A conscientious teacher will invest the time and energy needed to perform well in the new setting; but even under favorable conditions, teachers will require time to accommodate such changes. When the context of teaching changes (the level, the content, or the environment), an experienced teacher can become, in effect, a novice.

Other Measurement Issues

In defining what good teaching is, evaluators must address issues of weighting, standard setting, and "score" combining.

Weighting. Are all the evaluative criteria equally important? Or are some more important than others? Would educators in a district determine that *establishing an environment of respect and rapport,* for example, is more important than *contributing to the school and district?* Alternatively, are some evaluative criteria more important in some settings than in others? For example, is it critical for primary teachers to know the resources available to them for their teaching, but less important for high school teachers to do so? Or, if it is critical for novice teachers to be evaluated on the quality of their routines and procedures, can these skills be assumed in more experienced teachers? We discuss these issues more fully in Chapter 9.

Score Combining. Can excellent performance in one area compensate for inadequate performance in another? In other words, can

evaluators "average" scores? If a teacher were found to be deficient in a particular aspect of teaching, or in an entire domain, could this poor performance be compensated by excellent performance in another aspect of teaching? For example, could high ratings in the classroom environment compensate for low ratings in preparation and planning? Or would this inadequacy be sufficient to lead to the intensive assistance phase or even to nonrenewal? Alternatively, should the scores on the different aspects of teaching be "added together" in some way to obtain a total "score," with a certain total required for movement to the tenured status, or for a "satisfactory" or "outstanding" overall rating?

Standard Setting. How good is good enough? Is an acceptable (or exemplary) level of performance the same for novice teachers as for career professionals? For example, is "basic" level performance adequate for first- and second-year teachers, but not for attaining career (or tenured) status? Must teachers demonstrate a certain level of performance in each component of a domain, or only in a certain number (or percentage) of them? Any number of decision rules are possible here and are related to the prior discussion about score combining. One possibility is to require a certain level of performance in each component, or to permit only a certain number of "basic" ratings within a domain, or overall, to earn an overall rating of "satisfactory" or "outstanding."

Context Considerations

In establishing criteria for teacher evaluation, schools and districts should not be too rigid or formulaic. In particular, they should not confuse criteria with desired kinds of behavior. For example, the way in which a primary teacher establishes an environment of respect and rapport in the classroom will be fundamentally different from the way a high school teacher gets respect and establishes rapport. That is, the specific behavior each employs will be different, as appropriate to the different students they teach and the different context in which they work. Moreover, even with the same teacher in the same subject (for example, high school biology), the manner in which the skills are displayed may be quite different in the different environments. The third-period class, for example, might be very different from the general biology class that meets during seventh period. However, the effect created in the different classes is the same: Every student feels respected; every student feels valued; every student feels that it is a safe environment in which to take intellectual risks. Therefore, when an evaluation system is constructed on a framework of teaching skills, it must be understood by everyone that the aspects of teaching described in the framework do not refer to specific kinds of behavior (these will vary by teachers and according to the context) but rather to the underlying concepts.

Last, a single set of evaluative criteria is unlikely to be suitable to all those individuals in a school who are included in the teachers' contract. They are typically written with the classroom teacher in mind, the teacher who holds the primary responsibility for a group of 20–30 students for periods of time ranging from 40 minutes to six hours. But what about the resource teacher, who works with individuals or small groups, either in the regular classroom or in another setting? What about the speech teacher? The media or technology specialist? The school nurse? The counselor? These variations on the "teacher's" role must be

accommodated in the definition of teaching embodied in the evaluative criteria. Some school districts have worked from a consistent definition of teaching, such as that in *Enhancing Professional Practice: A Framework for Teaching* (Danielson, 1996), and have made necessary additions and substitutions to arrive at an equivalent definition of teaching for teachers who work in nonclassroom settings. These efforts serve to define those roles and to engage those directly involved in determining what is most important about their jobs.

For example, the media specialists in Downer's Grove, Illinois, have created a framework for their roles similar to Danielson's (1996) framework for teaching. Figure 4.2 shows their "framework for librarians," and Figure 4.3 contains one example of their descriptions of levels of performance, that from Component C3: Assisting Teachers.

"Outputs," or the Results Teachers Achieve

In addition to defining good teaching in terms of what teachers do, an evaluation system can base its evaluation of teachers on the results they achieve with students, in terms of their learning. Those advocating such a course of action maintain that it does not matter much what teachers do if their actions do not result in student learning; student success is the essential "bottom line."

Recent research findings have demonstrated that the quality of teaching matters—a lot. Reflecting what parents have known for years, the teacher to whom a student is assigned can have an enormous effect on the nature of students' experiences in school and the amount

FIGURE 4.2
Framework for Librarians
Community High School District 99, Downers Grove, Illinois

Library Domain A: Instructional Consultant

A1: Participating in curriculum development and assessment program
  Incorporation of information literacy into the curriculum
  Consultation

A2: Collaborating with individual teachers
  Planning process
  Identification of resources
  Learning activities

A3: Providing leadership in instructional technology
  Dissemination of information on new educational devlopments
  Leadership in using new technologies

Library Domain B: Classroom Instructor

B1: Planning instruction
  Knowledge of content and pedagogy
  Learning activities
  Lesson structure

B2: Learning environment
  Environment of respect and rapport
  Culture for learning
  Expectations for learning and achievement
  Classroom procedures
  Student behavior

B3: Instruction
  Communicating directions and procedures
  Questioning and discussion techniques
  Presentation of content
  Structure and pacing
  Flexibility and responsiveness

Library Domain C: Information Specialist

C1: Providing resources
  Selection of materials and equipment
  Promotion of new resources
  Incorporation of resources beyond the library

C2: Assisting students
  Guidance in information literacy
  Support for independent learning
  Promotion of social responsibility

C3: Assisting teachers
  Promotion of information resources
  Facilitation of technology

Library Domain D: Professional Responsibilities

D1: Reflecting on librarianship
  Accuracy of reflection
  Use for future behavior

D2: Maintaining accurate records
  Accuracy
  Timeliness
  Comprehensiveness

D3: Contributing to the school and district
  Relationships with colleagues
  Service to the school
  Participation in school and district projects
  Commitment to the institution

D4: Growing and developing professionally
  Enhancement of content knowledge and pedagogical skill
  Service to the profession

D5: Showing professionalism
  Service to students
  Advocacy
  Decision-making

		FIGURE 4.3		
		Levels of Performance		

Library Domain C: Information Specialist
Component C3: Assisting Teachers
Elements: Promotion of information resources
Facilitation of technology

Element	Unsatisfactory	Basic	Proficient	Distinguished
Promotion of information resources	Librarian fails to suggest appropriate resources and formats to meet instructional objectives.	Librarian suggests a limited range of appropriate resources and formats to meet instructional objectives.	Librarian encourages the use of a broad range of appropriate resources and formats to meet instructional objectives.	Librarian promotes the use of a broad range of appropriate resources and formats to meet instructional objectives.
Facilitation of technology	Librarian fails to evaluate, select, and manage technologies and instruct teachers on their use.	Librarian sometimes evaluates, selects, and manages technologies and instructs teachers on their use.	Librarian evaluates, selects, and manages technologies and instructs teachers on their use.	Librarian demonstrates knowledge of a full range of technologies and advocates their incorporation into planning with teachers.

students learn (Archer, 1998). For example, school officials in Dallas, Texas, analyzing the effect of different teachers on student learning, found that the average math scores of a group of 4th graders who were assigned to three highly effective teachers in a row rose from the 59th percentile in the 4th grade to the 76th percentile by the end of 6th grade. The comparable scores for another group of 4th graders, assigned to three ineffective teachers in a row, were the 60th percentile in 4th grade, but only the 27th percentile by the end of 6th grade. This difference in three years (49 percentile points, for students who began at roughly the same level) is highly significant and could make the difference between a successful secondary school career and an unsuccessful one. Similar results—with differences in learning of 35 percentile points—were found in reading (Jordan, Mendro, & Weesinghe, cited in Haycock, 2000). The results of another study, from Tennessee, also show striking results: Achievement gains shown by 5th graders in mathematics were 83 percent for those students with three consecutive very effective teachers compared with 29 percent for those with three consecutive ineffective teachers—a difference of more than 50 points (Sanders & Rivers, 1996).

Given the research findings on the effect of individual teachers on the learning of students, most educators acknowledge that student learning is relevant to the evaluation of teachers. The quality of teaching, in other words, is highly significant to the degree of student learning. The challenge, for both educators and policymakers, is how to capture and use information on student learning—and, indeed, deciding what information is most relevant. This is one of the most complex issues surrounding teacher evaluation, and the one most likely to generate lively political debate. The factors involved include assessment issues, outside influences on students, and characteristics of the school system itself.

Should standardized test scores be used, or performance on state tests? But what about those subjects—for example, music—or those grade levels for which standards do not exist? And what about those aspects of a school's curriculum—for example, writing—that do not lend themselves to traditional testing at all?

The Assessment of Student Learning

Approaches to teacher evaluation that incorporate a measure of student learning require valid techniques to assess that learning. That is, if we assume that student learning is a valid indicator of the quality of teaching, then we expect valid measures of that learning to be available. Unfortunately, valid measures are far from assured. Traditionally, school districts have relied on nationally normed, multiple-choice, machine-scorable tests of basic skills produced by test publishers, such as the Stanford Achievement Test, the Iowa Test of Basic Skills, or the Metropolitan Achievement Test. The use of these tests makes large-scale monitoring of student progress possible, and may be organized by cross-section (for example, 3rd grade scores from one year compared with the

3rd grade scores from a different year, demonstrating trends in performance with different groups of students). Alternatively, the same test scores make it possible to track performance of a "cohort" of students, for example, the scores of this year's 4th graders examined against those of last year's 3rd graders, to show the progress made in one year by the same group of students. But inherent in either of these approaches is the assumption that the tests used accurately reflect what teachers taught in school.

This assumption is debatable. Multiple-choice tests can assess only certain types of content, primarily knowledge of facts and procedures. They are far less suited to testing other, more complex forms of learning, such as students' ability to solve nonroutine problems, write an essay, or design an experiment. Norm-referenced, standardized tests, in other words, are well suited to measuring student learning if one subscribes to the paradigm of teacher as transmitter of knowledge and students as passive recipients. But they are less suited to the more recently accepted, complex content standards in place in many states and school districts. That is, it is impossible to assess, *through traditional testing methods*, many aspects of student learning regarded as important, particularly in the Information Age.

Many states have recently designed their own assessments for evaluating student learning. These vary widely. Some are similar to those available from commercial vendors; others engage students in more complex performance tasks and collections of work in a portfolio. These large-scale assessments raise many measurement challenges (for example, can evaluators validly assess a student's skill in writing on the basis of a single essay?). School administrators need to be aware of the issues before they accept the results of statewide tests as valid, absolute measures of student achievement, rather than as indicators.

An alternative is to use classroom assessments developed by teachers as measures of student learning. Such tests will probably reflect what the teachers actually taught. But this practice introduces other difficulties. Classroom assessments are unlikely to be comparable from one teacher to another. Any student can tell you that some teachers are more demanding than others, and administer more challenging tests. And it is unlikely that all teachers' tests, even if they are of comparable difficulty, would equally assess the district's content standards. Moreover, the tests might be administered under different conditions, with some teachers offering more assistance and coaching than others.

Influences on Student Learning

Student learning is highly influenced by factors beyond the control of the school. Some students' lives are much more difficult and isolated than those of other students, particularly if they are responsible for caring for younger siblings or assisting with earning money for the family. Some family members are much better equipped (through their own experiences or the resources at their disposal) to support their children academically. They are able to provide a quiet location for schoolwork and to offer assistance when needed. They can take weekend excursions to local places of interest and provide a home environment (through dinner-table conversation and bedtime reading, for example) that promotes learning. Further, some families simply *expect* their children to continue their education beyond high school

and, through their understanding of this process, can help their children make an informed decision. Student backgrounds—far from equitable—greatly influence the level of student performance.

Schools as Systems

Even within the school, the situation is complicated. Schools are complex systems, and the instructional skill of individual teachers is only one factor, though an important one, influencing student learning. Other factors are the curriculum, the school orgaization, and the type of learning support the school offers. For example, if a teacher is assigned a group of algebra students, but half of them don't understand fractions, that teacher's results on the end-of-year test will not be as good as those from another class in which the students entered well prepared. This teacher may have done an excellent job of teaching mathematics, and may have taught "a year's worth" of the curriculum. She may have clarified the students' misconceptions and given them a solid foundation for next year's math content. It is questionable, however, whether this teacher should be held accountable for the success of students in a curriculum (e.g., algebra) for which the students did not have the prerequisite knowledge.

In addition, the characteristics of students assigned to a teacher will influence that teacher's level of performance. Some students learn more quickly than others; and classes with large numbers of second-language learners, special needs students, or students with poor prior learning pose particular challenges for teachers. If an accountability system includes the level of student achievement, district evaluators should apply it to the school as a whole, rather than the performance of individual teachers.

The Concept of "Value-Added"

If the district uses measures of student achievement in the evaluation of individual teachers, the system should take into account the baseline levels of student achievement. This practice—the evaluation of teaching performance based not on the absolute level of performance of students, but on the amount they learn as the result of the teacher's efforts—is behind the concept of "value-added." This has advantages over looking at the absolute level of performance, but presents some of its own difficulties.

Some of these difficulties are similar to those that apply to absolute levels of performance; for example, the advantages that some students enjoy in their home environments affect not only their absolute levels of achievement, but their rate of learning. In addition, depending on how schools collect the data, a teacher could appear "ineffective" if a good student moved away in the middle of the year, or if students who were difficult to teach moved in.

The concept of "value-added" as a criterion of teacher performance presents yet another difficult challenge to those who design evaluation systems. Every school contains some students who are more challenging to teach than others, arising from either cognitive or behavioral characteristics (for example, poor proficiency in English, poor prior learning, or an impoverished home environment). If an evaluation system depends too rigidly on demonstrated student growth, the system will create a disincentive for teachers to teach those students who present the most difficult challenges. Designers must ensure that the system,

in effect, does not penalize teachers for taking on difficult instructional challenges.

As educators and the public recognize the importance of teacher quality, state and district policy will require attention to student achievement in teacher evaluation. Indeed, the state of Delaware has recently ruled that student learning shall be an integral part of the evaluation of teachers. In designing systems for teacher evaluation, however, schools and districts must find fair ways to measure student learning. The technical issues involved are significant, and school and district planners need to address and resolve these issues before they implement a high-stakes system.

Other Approaches

As part of a "value-added" system, evaluators could ask teachers to provide evidence of learning by students in their charge. For example, a 5th grade teacher could submit writing samples of students in her class from September and May. Similarly, a teacher could submit examples of student problem solving from different points during the year. If such an approach is to be effective, the student work should be representative of the class as a whole (not just the most advanced students, for example), and the types of learning demonstrated should represent important content, for example, progress on the state content standards. Though presenting certain challenges, such an approach has the advantage of avoiding most of the technical difficulties with relying on tests of student achievement, while preserving attention to the most important aspect of a teacher's work, namely whether the students are actually learning.

In one interesting approach, embodied in the "Teacher Work Sample" methodology, teachers assess their students on a curriculum standard and create an instructional unit to support that standard. They then teach the unit and administer both pre- and post-assessments on the content. The learning gains demonstrated by students (frequently disaggregated by ability groups) provides a measure of the teacher's effectiveness.

Although this approach avoids the difficulties of relying on external measures of student learning, it presents its own challenges. For example, it assumes that teachers can design (or select) valid assessment measures for both pre- and post-assessments, ones that assess the knowledge and skills identified in the unit. Further, it assumes that the two assessments are roughly equivalent in difficulty—that they comprise alternate "forms" of a test. And even if the assessments are valid measures of student learning, the approach lends itself more to certain types of learning than to others, such as knowledge and procedural skill. For other instructional goals—for example, writing or problem-solving skills—progress is often difficult to document over a short period of time. Evaluating students' writing skills or problem-solving abilities requires assessment more sophisticated than a "test." So although the work sample methodology respects the idea that teachers are uniquely responsible for the learning of their students, it should not be used alone.

Last, evaluators can ask teachers to provide other evidence of student engagement in their learning, for example, improved student attendance, higher rates of student completion of assignments, or increased participation in class discussions. These types of evidence are not direct measures of improved student learning, but they are clearly relevant and can serve as indicators of student engagement that are likely to contribute to student learning.

☙ ☙ ☙

As this chapter shows, people have differing conceptions of the "what" of teaching—the criteria used in an evaluation system. These criteria can include what teachers do, the tasks of teaching, or what Michael Scriven (1988, 1994) calls "duties." Alternatively, schools might organize the evaluative criteria according to the results teachers achieve or the degree of student learning they cause. The latter approach has both obvious appeal (student learning is, after all, the mission of schools) and enormous technical difficulties (it is virtually impossible to devise an equitable system). It seems prudent to include both approaches in a well-balanced evaluation of teaching—examining teaching practice for the skill teachers demonstrate and considering the degree of student learning they produce.

5

Sources of Information

If a teacher evaluation system is to be valid, schools and districts must develop a definition of teaching (evaluative criteria) and then use instruments and procedures to assess teachers according to those criteria. Any evaluation system requires that teachers do certain things: For example, they may allow administrators or peers to observe them while teaching, they may complete a portfolio of lesson plans, they may submit letters they have written to parents. Taken together, what teachers do as part of the evaluation procedures should provide evidence of all the evaluative criteria. For example, if "establishing an environment of respect and rapport" is included as an essential criterion of teaching, then how will teachers demonstrate their skill? How should teachers organize their procedures to enable an evaluator to judge their classroom environment?

Some teaching standards are written in such a manner that they cannot be evaluated reliably. This relates to the fact that only behavior can be assessed. States of mind, beliefs, values, and some kinds of knowledge are invisible until they are revealed in behavior. Consider, for example, the NBPTS standard: The teacher is "committed to students and their learning."

Although no one would disagree with the values embodied in such as statement, how can teachers validly demonstrate such a commitment? There would be indicators, to be sure (for example, a teacher might go to considerable lengths to locate alternative materials for a student needing them, or tutor students during the lunch period). But the commitment itself is a mental state that evaluators can only infer from the teacher's actions.

Some of the evaluative criteria, no doubt, are of the type that a principal or a peer might observe in the classroom during a teaching episode. An observer could determine whether the environment in the classroom was a respectful one, both between the teacher and the students and among the students. Or an observer could analyze the questions the teacher asked for their level of cognitive challenge.

But other possible criteria (such as communicating with families, or collaborating with colleagues) are invisible in the classroom; these criteria require other types of documentation. How can teachers demonstrate their skill in *all* the diverse aspects of the complex activity of teaching? What would count as evidence, and how should it be evaluated?

Consider the Evidence

Though it may sound legalistic, the concept of evidence is important in this regard. How can teachers provide evidence of their skill in the different components of teaching? Which are demonstrated through classroom interaction, and which require additional, or alternate, evidence? If the evaluative criteria include measures of student learning, what would count as evidence? And how can it be collected in an equitable manner? In addition, who should provide or collect the evidence? And how can schools and districts design a system that yields evidence of all the components of teaching—and that still enhances the engagement and professional learning of teachers?

In traditional evaluation systems, an administrator collects all evidence of teaching skill during a classroom episode. The teacher conducts a lesson, which the administrator observes, taking notes (sometimes with the stated goal of recording "everything" that happens). The administrator then "writes up" the observation (which is sometimes called an *evaluation*) and meets with the teacher to provide feedback to the teacher on the observed lesson and the teacher's skill as demonstrated in that lesson.

In such a traditional system, the teacher is essentially passive; it is the administrator who conducts the observation, takes notes, and summarizes those notes against the evaluative criteria. The administrator conducts the observation and the evaluation and then provides feedback to the teacher about her teaching.

Recent findings (initially based on teachers' reports of the certification process for the NBPTS, and more recently based on their experiences in newly developed district evaluation systems) have suggested that schools and districts enhance professional learning when teachers themselves play a larger and more active role in the evaluation process. For example, they can conduct a self-assessment, collect documents from a lesson (plans, instructional artifacts, student work), and then describe the practice to the evaluator. Although the administrator and the teacher may disagree about a particular aspect of teaching (and it is the evaluator's judgment that, in the end, must prevail), the professional conversation is likely to be rich, and the teacher may indeed convince the administrator of her point of view.

When an evaluation system adopts a complex view of teaching, one based on teacher decision-making to promote student learning, it is essential to capture that decision-making in the evaluation procedures. And if the definition of teaching is comprehensive and includes skills such as designing coherent instruction or communicating with families—beyond what may be demonstrated in classroom interaction—other sources of evidence are needed.

The idea of a professional portfolio, assembled and presented as part of an evaluation system, has gained popularity in recent years. Indeed, such an effort can offer a significant vehicle for professional reflection on practice. However, before jumping into requiring a portfolio as part of an evaluation system, those designing the system should be very clear about the evaluative criteria for which they want teachers to provide evidence, and to use those criteria when setting the specifications for the portfolio.

What sources of information, then, are possible? We suggest that they include classroom observations, but go beyond observation to teacher self-assessments, planning documents, analysis of student work, and other sources of evidence.

Classroom Observation

In many schools and districts, teacher evaluation is synonymous with classroom observation. Indeed, a classroom observation is the best, and the only, setting in which to witness essential aspects of teaching—for example, the interaction between teacher and students and among students. An astute observer can note how the teacher structures the physical environment, how the teacher engages students in learning, how he establishes and maintains standards of conduct.

Of course, a videotape of a class can provide much of the same information. Videotapes are used as part of the certification process for the NBPTS. And for purposes of formative assessment and analysis, the use of videotape has many advantages. Teachers in a study group can learn much from watching a videotape of one of the members; they can pause the tape at any time to discuss the lesson, to learn what the teacher was thinking and planning at different points, and to replay sections.

For evaluation purposes in a school setting, however, where teachers and administrators are in the same location, live observation is far better than videotaping. A videotape is a very poor substitute for direct observation. For one thing, with a tape, a viewer can see only what the camera captures; when conducting a live observation, one can note peripheral events and can scan the room at any point to notice, for example, students' reactions to events. In addition, live observation allows an observer to note the "feel" of a class, the climate that is not always communicated through a video camera.

Classroom observation is a critical evaluation methodology for those aspects of teaching that may be directly observed. Some important aspects of instruction, however—even those involving a teacher's work with students, such as providing feedback to students—are not necessarily easily observed in a classroom episode. Feedback to students might be better documented by looking at a teacher's comments on student papers, or by listening in on a teacher conference with an individual student. Similarly, a teacher's skill in establishing classroom routines may not be observed directly, but rather inferred from the behavior of students as they go about their business, seemingly with no direction from the teacher.

Teacher Self-assessment

Teachers are highly perceptive of their own skills in teaching, and are, or can become, extremely accurate in their perceptions. Further, the act of self-assessment requires reflection, an activity documented through research to yield professional learning and growth. Self-assessment may be incorporated into either the formal evaluation process, or a process for self-directed professional growth, or both. As a source of information, self-assessment can add much to the dialogue regarding the quality of teaching.

When a district's system for teacher evaluation includes evaluative criteria with clear descriptions of levels of performance (see Danielson, 1996), teachers can examine their teaching against those descriptions and determine their relative strengths and weaknesses. The specificity provided in such a system is an encouragement for teachers to examine their practice, and to consider what evidence they might produce to substantiate their self-assessment.

Structured Reflection

It is now well recognized that few activities promote professional learning as effectively as structured reflection on practice. This phenomenon accounts for the experience of many candidates for NBPTS certification, who report that preparing their portfolios was an extremely rich professional endeavor. But many teachers don't take the time to reflect in a systematic manner unless specifically asked to do so. That is, although many teachers think about their teaching and what they might have done to improve student learning, they frequently don't engage in a formal process of reflection and rarely commit their reflections to writing. When teachers take the time to pause and consider their work systematically, however, they are richly rewarded. The very act of reflection, it appears, is a highly productive vehicle for professional learning. A teacher evaluation system, then, committed to maximizing the professional growth of teachers, should include a focused approach to structured reflection on practice.

Planning Documents

Planning is an important skill in its own right, distinct from a teacher's ability to conduct a successful instructional experience for students. Planning requires thoughtful consideration of what students should learn; the nature of the subject; the background, interests, and skills of the learners; and how to engage students in a meaningful way with the content. Skilled planning requires a thorough knowledge of the subject, but such knowledge is insufficient. Teachers also need knowledge of content-specific pedagogy—how to engage students meaningfully and in increasingly complex ways with the content.

For instance, a teacher may note that the appropriate ways to sequence activities in developing a topic with students may not be the same as the logical progression of the same topic. Here's an example: If a teacher wanted sixth-grade students to understand the concepts of buoyancy and density, the logical approach might call for defining the terms, and providing examples of them, and possibly presenting the mathematical formulas for deriving them. A more developmental approach, on the other hand, might begin with presenting an anomaly to students, an enigma for which there is no easy explanation. For example, "Why is it that battleships, which are made of steel, will float?" Students could then explore that question, possibly using other materials, such as clay, to determine what factors cause a substance to float or sink. The teacher might then help students generalize these principles to encompass buoyancy and density. In developing a viable plan with such a sequence of learning experiences, the teacher would have to consider the students, their backgrounds, the specific learning objectives, and the available resources.

Planning is explicitly included as an entire domain (one of four) in the definition of good teaching in *Enhancing Professional Practice: A Framework for Teaching* (Danielson, 1996). Similarly, in most other definitions of teacher skill, such as those of the California Standards for the Teaching Profession, planning is identified as a critical aspect of performance. It is frequently tied to the teacher's deep knowledge of the content to be taught. The challenge for an evaluation system, then, is to determine how to ask teachers to document the skill of planning.

Unit plans and individual lesson plans provide evidence of long-range and short-term planning, and they may be evaluated independently of classroom performance. Does a unit plan, for example, project a coherent approach to a topic? Do the activities for students engage them in conceptual understanding? Do they represent appropriate variety and the best that we know regarding how students learn that discipline? Evaluators may answer these questions by studying planning documents and analyzing them against the evaluative criteria and their accompanying levels of performance.

Of course, teachers may display evidence of poor planning during a classroom observation if the materials they use are poorly aligned with the purpose of a lesson, or if the teachers demonstrate ignorance of important aspects of the content being taught. However, planning involves a complex set of skills and is independent of a teacher's skill in implementing those plans; some teachers, for example, may be good at planning, and less skilled at carrying plans out. Alternatively, a teacher's plans might be thoughtful and imaginative, but inappropriate for a particular group of students.

Planning, both short-term and long-range, must be goal-directed, supporting student learning that is both significant and aligned with state or local content standards. It must reflect the levels of learning and backgrounds of the students and incorporate elements of active learning. Further, plans must be coherent and should include strategies for assessment of student learning.

Teaching Artifacts

Students experience their teachers' skill not only in their direct interaction; they also encounter artifacts created or selected by their teachers, such as assignments, worksheets, and project directions. In fact, it is estimated that over half of students' school experiences is a function of the "stuff" created or selected by teachers. Such artifacts, then, represent an important aspect of teacher performance and can be assessed as part of an evaluation system.

When teaching artifacts are included in a system for evaluation, they provide a window into classroom life not accessible through planning documents alone. By reading what a teacher is asking students to do, an evaluator can appreciate (at least vicariously) the cognitive challenge required by the task and the level of intellectual engagement by students the teacher expected. And if the teacher includes brief commentary to accompany the materials, such as responses to questions about the purpose of the activity, and how she intends for students' understanding to be advanced, the evaluator can get a hint of the teacher's thinking.

These artifacts provide evidence not only of classroom life and of the teacher's thinking, but of the teacher's skill in planning. Artifacts, combined with classroom observations, enable an evaluator to witness a teacher's plans coming to life for students. In addition, the artifacts can demonstrate how a teacher has adapted the assignments to the needs of individuals or groups of students within the class.

Other Evidence

Some aspects of a teacher's performance do not lend themselves to evidence provided by classroom observation, planning documents, or instructional artifacts. If the evaluative criteria include other aspects of professionalism, these will require other forms of evidence altogether. How does a teacher demonstrate skill in communicating with families, for example, or in contributing to the school and district?

Parent and Community Communications

Class newsletters, curriculum outlines for back-to-school night, student progress reports, logs of parent contacts, notes from parent conferences, and information regarding a planned school excursion are all examples of evidence of a teacher's skill in communicating with families. Teachers might collect these items and present them as part of a professional portfolio for evaluation.

Logs of Professional Development Activities and School or District Projects

Many teachers contribute to the professional life of their schools and districts—and to the teaching profession—in a variety of ways. They may organize the spelling bee, or serve on the site council, or make a presentation at a local conference. Most teachers, however, don't think to record these contributions, nor to submit evidence of them as part of the evaluation process. Logs, supplemented by artifacts like conference programs or documents produced by a committee, provide important evidence of teachers' active engagement in the professional life of the school or district and their commitment to their own professional growth.

Samples of Student Work or Other Evidence of Student Learning

Schools and districts are increasingly evaluating teachers on the learning of their students. It does not matter, the argument goes, what teachers *do*, if the students are not learning well. Many evaluation systems are requiring teachers to submit evidence of their effect on student learning and progress.

Standardized test scores, of course, provide one indication of student learning. As noted in Chapter 4, however, schools and districts should use such measures cautiously to demonstrate the effectiveness of individual teachers. On the other hand, student work can provide direct evidence of student learning and achievement; and teachers should select samples of student work to represent the full range of ability and skill in a class. If collected over time, particularly from the same students, student work can demonstrate growth in skill and conceptual learning. And if accompanied by a brief commentary by the teacher, it can reveal the teacher's skill in diagnostic assessment and planning for future learning.

As noted previously, evaluation systems based on the use of standardized achievement data in systems of teacher evaluation present technical challenges and are difficult to implement fairly. Asking teachers to provide evidence of the learning of students in their own classes avoids some of the technical measurement difficulties and offers teachers the opportunity to demonstrate their instructional skill as manifested in improved student performance.

Student, Parent, or Colleague Feedback

Evaluation systems that incorporate the perspectives of others, in addition to a teacher's direct supervisor, are called 360-degree systems. Such systems are based on the idea that an educator's skill may be seen from several different perspectives and that it should be exemplary (or at least adequate) from all those different angles. Used extensively in the business world, this approach has much to offer educational evaluation as well, with formal evaluations supplemented by, for example, observations from colleagues on a teaching team or on a curriculum committee, or parent or student surveys.

Just as teachers, office staff, and cafeteria workers see aspects of a principal's performance that might not be visible to the superintendent of schools (the principal's supervisor), students, parents, and colleagues can provide evidence of a teacher's performance that a principal might never witness. If districts or schools use such feedback, however, the designers of the evaluation system need to exercise caution so that such information is valid and not compromised by personality differences, favoritism, or other irrelevant matters.

Surveys of parents and students can provide a great deal of information. Though simple in concept, such surveys are not easy to design.

- *Student surveys* must be appropriate to the age of the students and should ask questions about the class, rather than about the teacher. For example, the survey could ask students to agree or disagree (or indicate intermediate points on a continuum) with such statements as "All students are treated fairly in this class," or "I always know what I am expected to do for

assignments in this class." The survey should include only questions that students are actually in a position to answer. Young children, in particular, would not be able to comment on the teacher's level of content expertise or the extent to which the instructional strategies used were suitable to the content. Figure 5.1 is an example of a student survey (see p. 52).

- *Parent surveys* should pose questions that parents can reasonably answer and should not be excessively detailed. For example, parents would have no way of knowing whether teachers presented lessons in a manner in which students could understand. They would know, however, whether their own children had the skills they needed to complete homework assignments or whether they themselves could understand communications from their child's teacher. They could also comment on whether the teacher was accessible to them when they needed to contact that teacher or whether the teacher returned phone calls promptly. Figure 5.2 (p. 52) shows a sample parent survey.

Surveys can offer highly valuable insights into a teacher's performance, and they can provide feedback to teachers that is unavailable from any other source. Because they are based on perceptions, however, evaluators should not consider parent and student surveys as *entirely* reliable sources of evidence. At their best, they can be used for formative feedback and to supplement other indicators of teacher performance.

In addition to the evidence described in this chapter, other indicators of a teacher's performance are a matter of school records. For example, some teachers send many more students than do others to the office for discipline

FIGURE 5.1 Sample Student Survey (Middle or High School Students)				
Statement	**Strongly Disagree**	**Disagree**	**Agree**	**Strongly Agree**
I understand what I am supposed to do in class and for homework.				
I understand the rules in this class.				
If I need help, I feel comfortable asking for assistance.				
Students in this class usually pay attention to the teacher and to one another.				
All students are treated fairly in this class.				
This class is interesting because we don't do the same things every day.				
Students know that they can't get away with things in this class.				
This teacher cares about whether I learn the material.				

FIGURE 5.2 Sample Parent Survey				
Statement	**Strongly Disagree**	**Disagree**	**Agree**	**Strongly Agree**
This teacher treats my child fairly and with respect.				
My child has the skills to complete his or her homework.				
This teacher keeps me informed of my child's progress in school.				
My child appears to know what is expected by this teacher.				
This teacher uses a fair grading system.				

FIGURE 5.3
Sources of Information

Component of the Framework	Sample Sources of Information
Domain 1: Planning and Preparation	
1a: Demonstrating Knowledge of Content and Pedagogy	Classroom observation, sample unit plan, sample lesson plan, interview, log
1b: Demonstrating Knowledge of Students	Interviews, sample lesson plan
1c: Selecting Instructional Goals	Sample unit plan, sample lesson plan, teaching artifact
1d: Demonstrating Knowledge of Resources	Sample unit plan, sample lesson plan
1e: Designing Coherent Instruction	Sample unit plan, sample lesson plan, teaching artifact
1f: Assessing Student Learning	Sample unit plan, sample lesson plan, teaching artifact
Domain 2: The Classroom Environment	
2a: Creating an Environment of Respect and Rapport	Classroom observation; student surveys; parent surveys
2b: Establishing a Culture for Learning	Classroom observation, teaching artifact, samples of student work; student surveys; parent surveys
2c: Managing Classroom Procedures	Classroom observation, interview
2d: Managing Student Behavior	Classroom observation, interview, records of students sent to the office
2e: Organizing Physical Space	Classroom observation
Domain 3: Instruction	
3a: Communicating Clearly and Accurately	Classroom observation
3b: Using Questioning and Discussion Techniques	Classroom observation
3c: Engaging Students in Learning	Classroom observation, teaching artifact, samples of student work
3d: Providing Feedback to Students	Classroom observation, samples of student work
3e: Demonstrating Flexibility and Responsiveness	Classroom observation
Domain 4: Professional Responsibilities	
4a: Reflecting on Teaching	Interview, reflection form
4b: Maintaining Accurate Records	Attendance records, field trip records
4c: Communicating with Families	Phone logs, letters to parents, back-to-school night handouts, parent survey, phone calls from parents
4d: Contributing to the School and District	Logs of professional activities; copies of documents to which teacher has contributed, with explanation of role
4e: Growing and Developing Professionally	Logs of professional goals and improved practice; copies of conference programs attended or at which presented
4f: Showing Professionalism	Interview, feedback from colleagues

referrals; some teachers generate spontaneous and admiring comments from parents; some teachers willingly accept additional responsibilities around the school, whereas others avoid them. All these matters, and others like them, can offer important, albeit indirect, evidence of a teacher's overall performance.

Sources-of-Information Chart

So how can designers of evaluation systems match the different sources of information to the evaluation criteria? It is essentially a matter of common sense, as Figure 5.3 demonstrates.

Figure 5.3 (p. 53) identifies the principal sources of evidence for each of the components of Danielson's (1996) *Enhancing Professional*

Practice: A Framework for Teaching. If evaluators use other criteria, they would need to adjust the chart accordingly.

As outlined in this chapter, educators may use various sources of evidence to document the different aspects of performance defined in the established definition of exemplary practice. And although all these sources of evidence serve important evaluation functions, some of them, in addition, engage teachers in valuable professional learning. When evaluation systems allow teachers to choose between different sources, teachers should select those that have the greatest potential for professional learning.

6

Evaluation Procedures, or the "How"

Evaluation procedures are those methods (the "how") that teachers use to document or demonstrate their skills and knowledge (the "what," or the criteria of good teaching). The "how" and the "what," of course, must be aligned. For every aspect of performance deemed essential to good practice, teachers must have a way to document their skill. Developing assessments that are valid and reliable demands that we devote serious attention to the procedural aspects of evaluation.

Many educators have discovered an even more compelling reason to design the procedures carefully. People learn from what they do; schools and districts can design evaluation procedures that provide opportunities for professional learning for teachers. That is, teachers may actually improve their practice by engaging in the activities required as part of the evaluation process.

We can pursue conversation and decisions regarding evaluation procedures on two levels: the general procedures and the detailed instruments and procedures.

General Procedures

Given the complexity of teaching and the long list of teaching skills (including, possibly, evidence of student learning), how, in general, will teachers demonstrate their skill? What will they do? Will the system include classroom observation? Will it include a professional portfolio? Will procedures for new teachers be different from those for veterans? Issues addressed here include differentiated procedures (for probationary and nonprobationary teachers), types of evaluation activities, time lines for evaluation activities, and personnel to be included.

Differentiated Procedures

Teaching, alone among the professions, makes the same demands on novices as on experienced practitioners. The moment first-year teachers enter their first classroom, they are held to the same standard and subjected to the same procedures as their more experienced colleagues.

Most other professions build in a period of apprenticeship. Doctors participate in internships and residencies, intensive experiences that prepare them for the rigors of independent practice. Accountants and architects are hired by firms, where they work—for a few years at least—under the close supervision of a veteran. But teachers are simply "thrown in the deep end," receiving little real assistance from other teachers in the school. In some cases, schools and districts assign them the most preparations, the most difficult students, and the least attractive room (or none at all) and leave them to "sink or swim." And when the principal arrives to conduct an observation, he uses the same procedures as those used with experienced teachers.

Teaching, however, has a distinct life cycle; teachers at different stages in their careers have different needs and different levels of skill. Novice teachers are engaged in rapid and intense learning and require a good deal of support in developing their basic teaching skills. Experienced teachers, on the other hand, have many of the routines of teaching under control and can devote energy and attention to refining their skill. Experienced, but struggling, teachers may have to reexamine their philosophy of education and their current practice in light of changing educational theory and changing student populations.

This life cycle suggests that nontenured (probationary) teachers, tenured (career) teachers, and teachers needing intensive assistance should participate in evaluation activities that are different from one another. Even if the evaluative criteria for novice and experienced teachers are the same, schools and districts should use different procedures for teachers at different stages in their careers. Some school districts using *Enhancing Professional Practice* (Danielson, 1996) as the source of the evaluative criteria have developed systems in which first-year teachers are evaluated on only 10 of the 22 components of teaching; 6 more components are added in the second year, and the final 6 components in the third year.

In creating differentiated procedures, some school districts have determined that all teachers participate in formal evaluation procedures,

with this difference: nontenured teachers and those experienced teachers in intensive assistance undergo this formal process every year, and tenured teachers participate in a formal evaluation process only every two, three, or four years. In addition, some districts, for example Coventry, Rhode Island, have determined that the length of time between formal evaluations varies according to how well a teacher performed in the last formal evaluation: The better the performance, the longer the time before the next one.

Further, those districts that require a formal evaluation process for career teachers only every two, three, or four years must determine what, in general, those teachers should do during the "other" years (they are careful not to call them the "off" years). In Newport News, Virginia, for example, teachers conduct a self-assessment and select, with their administrator, areas for focus. They then join a study group with colleagues, in which they pursue their focus areas, develop a plan, implement the plan, and reflect on the results. Then, when they undertake their formal evaluation in the fourth year, they submit samples of work done during the three "other" years as evidence of the evaluative criterion for professional growth. (See Appendix B for additional information about the Newport News approach to teacher evaluation.)

Types of Evaluation Activities

Classroom observation has long been a staple of the evaluation process, and it will always play an important role in the evaluation process. In many school districts, observation is virtually synonymous with evaluation. But it is only one type of evaluation activity, and it is not even suitable as a technique for gathering evidence about certain aspects of teaching, such as collaboration with colleagues. Other activities are possible, such as self-assessment and structured reflection, assembling of a professional portfolio, and surveys of students and parents. (Chapter 5 describes these activities in greater detail.)

Schools and districts select activities for an evaluation system primarily based on how they will provide evidence of the different evaluative criteria. That is, some aspects of teaching can only be demonstrated through classroom observation, whereas others require other types of evidence. Evaluation developers need to consider which activities will be suitable for documenting the different evaluative criteria.

Time Lines for Evaluation Activities

As part of designing an evaluation system, educators must determine not only what people must do as part of the process, but when they should do it. Each required activity should have a due date associated with it. The evaluation process should allow for certain internal and external deadlines and demands on educators' time, such as the following:

• *State or other contractual deadlines.* If teachers must be notified of their employment status before a certain date, the district process must enable evaluators to meet those deadlines.

• *School and district events.* Evaluation activities should not coincide with other time-consuming school or district events, such as back-to-school night, parent conferences, or final exams and grade reporting.

• *Administrative burden.* All evaluation systems make demands on administrators' time; but the evaluation committee can ensure that

the activities for the different phases of the process do not occur at the same time. For example, the schedule for required formal observations for probationary teachers should not coincide with conferences with nonprobationary teachers for goal setting.

Traditionally, the evaluation cycle begins in the fall after school has started (in August or September) and is completed in April or May of the following year. Some districts, however, are implementing different schedules, beginning in April of one year and finishing in March of the following year. Such a schedule fits well with most state requirements for notification of contract renewal or nonrenewal (typically in March or April). This schedule also enables teachers who are involved in a self-directed phase of the process to conduct a self-assessment in the spring and to write their professional growth plan toward the end of the school year. Then, if they are inclined to do so, they can make productive use of the summer months for professional development activities.

Evaluation Personnel

In traditional evaluation systems, supervisors or other administrators typically conduct the observations and write up the evaluations. But alternative approaches suggest that other educators might play a role in at least some of the required activities.

One important reason for extending the responsibility for evaluation activities beyond site administrators relates simply to time demands. Thoughtful evaluation requires a significant investment of time, and a single individual can devote that time to only a limited number of people. If the evaluation system uses a multiyear cycle for experienced teachers, and if teachers work together to conduct most of the evaluation activities required during the nonformal evaluation years, then site administrators are in a position to devote more time to the evaluations of probationary teachers, those experienced teachers scheduled for formal evaluations, and experienced teachers requiring intensive assistance.

Alternative evaluation personnel could include mentor teachers, department chairs, and central office personnel.

Mentors or Peer Coaches. In most school districts, mentors and coaches do not conduct teacher evaluations. The relationship between a teacher and an evaluator is usually different from that between a teacher and a coach or mentor, which requires a high level of trust and a safe environment for risk-taking. Both of these are more difficult to achieve in the threatening setting of evaluation. Teachers are unlikely to be candid in their professional discussions if they fear that the information could be used against them.

Mentors and peer coaches, however, can play an important role in the larger evaluation system. For example, if beginning teachers are evaluated every year by an administrator, they can also benefit from a mentoring relationship with a more experienced colleague, in which the mentor conducts formative assessments and provides feedback to the teacher. Here, the mentor would use the same evaluative criteria that the formal evaluation uses. Similarly, for experienced teachers, if the evaluation process includes several years of self-directed professional growth in between the years of formal evaluation, these activities are more productive if peers conduct them collaboratively. So although mentors and coaches may not conduct formal evaluations, they can play an

important role in the evaluation process in a collegial, nonjudgmental role.

Some districts have instituted the practice of peer review, or peer assistance and review. Peer review refers to a program in which teachers conduct formal, summative evaluation of their colleagues, in which their recommendations (sometimes in combination with recommendations from administrators) for an individual's employment status are typically accepted by the school district. Peer review is generally, though not exclusively, used with nontenured teachers. A peer assistance and review program combines peer assistance (formative assessment) and peer review (summative evaluation related to continuing employment status). Some schools and districts use this kind of program for new teachers or experienced teachers experiencing difficulties with their teaching. The primary purpose of these programs is to assist the teachers whose employment status may be threatened and to increase retention.

Peer assistance and review programs have been in place since the early 1980s in scattered locations around the United States (e.g., in Columbus and Toledo, Ohio; Rochester, New York; and Poway, California). Participants in these locations report improved instruction by participants and increased communication among all parties regarding instructional issues. Bob Chase (1997), president of the National Education Association, writes:

> In a successful peer-assistance and review program, teachers take charge of their own profession. They put professional development at the center of their local union's activities. They provide expert assistance to teachers who need help—often rescuing and revitalizing careers that would otherwise

collapse. And they also have the courage to counsel failing teachers to leave the profession in cases where sustained peer assistance is unavailing. Indeed, they view this self-policing as essential to the integrity of their profession (p. 29).

Further, some schools have found that when a teacher has left the profession while being supported by a peer assistance and review program, the teacher felt less diminished by the process than have some other departing teachers who were evaluated by administrators. The teachers' association generally manages the programs of peer review or peer assistance and review.

Department Chairs. In some schools, typically at the secondary level, department chairs are quasi-administrators in that they conduct teacher evaluations; in others, they teach full- or part-time and conduct administrative tasks, such as ordering supplies. In the different situations, their role in the evaluation system should be defined.

The participation of department chairs in the evaluation process has some important benefits. Because of their content expertise, such individuals are able to adequately assess content-specific pedagogy and other related aspects of a teacher's performance. This content-related assessment is more accurate than is possible for most administrators, who may have expertise in one curriculum area but rarely in all the subjects taught in a comprehensive high school. Further, the judgments of department heads will be more likely to be respected by the faculty, because they are closer to the instructional process than are most administrators and have taught (or are still teaching) in the same setting. On the other

hand, precisely because they are close to the realities of teaching, it may be more difficult for them to make suggestions regarding the performance of a colleague.

Central Office Administrators or Supervisors. The participation of central office administrators or supervisors in the evaluation process has many of the same advantages as that of department chairs, insofar as these individuals are typically expert in a discipline. Moreover, their participation has the additional advantage of not involving teachers in the evaluation of colleagues, as can occur when department chairs conduct evaluations.

There are disadvantages as well, to be sure. Central office administrators, particularly in large districts, because they are not based at the school site, may not be aware of the nuances of a school's culture that can affect teacher performance. In addition, they don't have the opportunities available to site administrators to observe teachers' work in informal or non-classroom settings, such as interactions with students or other teachers in school corridors or discussions in the teachers' lounge, faculty meetings, or parent conferences.

Therefore, it makes sense for administrators not based at the school site to participate in the teacher evaluation process by conducting some (but not all) of the classroom observations and evaluating planning documents, thereby contributing in the manner in which they are best qualified, namely, that of content expertise. District-level administrators, however, should not be asked to conduct a full evaluation, precisely because they are not located at the school site, and they can't be familiar with all the varied aspects of a teacher's performance.

Detailed Instruments and Procedures

It is insufficient to determine the general approaches to be used in the evaluation process; schools or districts implementing an evaluation system must develop the instruments and procedures in detail. *Exactly* what will teachers and administrators do, and when? What forms will they use, if any? If teachers are to write a commentary about student work, what questions should they answer?

The instruments and procedures used will depend on the evaluative criteria—and developers should consider issues like documentation, time available, equity, and professional development. The following sections address these issues.

Documentation

Taken together, the instruments and procedures should serve to document all the criteria; for every criterion identified as part of the "what," an accepted procedure must be available to teachers to demonstrate their skill. Further, the instruments and procedures should provide the opportunity for teachers to demonstrate performance at the highest level. For example, if the highest level of "growing and developing professionally" specifies that teachers conduct action research in their classrooms and share the results with colleagues, they must have the opportunity to do so.

Not Constitute an Unreasonable Burden

Procedures undertaken for an evaluation process should represent, to the extent possible, a "natural harvest" of teachers' work, rather than extra work that teachers must do solely for the evaluation process. If an evaluation process is overly burdensome, it will encourage teachers to cut corners, to go through the motions without investing cognitive energy into the work. If that happens, the entire process will become discredited and will be no improvement over the system it replaced. In addition, the process should consist of reasonable time lines and workloads for individuals, both teachers and administrators.

Even when developers carefully design evaluation activities to be as efficient as possible, an evaluation process will entail some extra work for teachers. But the requirements of the evaluation system should be, at most, an extension of what teachers do as a matter of course. That is, teachers usually plan their units and lessons carefully, and it is not a huge departure simply to write those plans down, at least once or twice a year, to accompany a formal observation. Teachers reflect on their lessons, and although they don't typically record their thoughts, doing so does not require a great deal of time. Teachers design instructional activities for their students, and they examine student work; to be asked to collect some of these and comment on them does not add significantly to the work of teaching. All these activities, though done in greater detail than many teachers would typically do them spontaneously, are not things they would not be doing, in some form, in any case.

Contribute to Professional Development

If well designed, the instruments and procedures used in an evaluation system can constitute valuable professional development for teachers, by, for example, encouraging self-assessment and reflection on practice. Indeed, it is one of the principal benefits of new systems of evaluation that the activities are worth doing in their own right, not merely as documentation of the evaluative criteria.

But this does not happen automatically; not all systems contribute to the professional learning of those involved. In developing the specific instruments and procedures, designers are well advised to attend to the characteristics of professional learning identified in Chapter 3. In general, activities that engage teachers in self-assessment and reflection on practice and activities that involve collaboration, will contribute to professional learning. This suggests that, to the extent possible, the teacher (rather than an administrator) should direct the evaluation activities. Evaluation should provide maximum opportunities for self-directed inquiry. The teacher, in other words, should play as active a role as possible.

Equity and Protection of Due Process

Naturally, instruments and procedures used in teacher evaluation should include assurances of due process and fundamental equity. The schedule must provide clearly stated, reasonable time lines. Procedures must be the same (or equivalent) for all, and there must be no trace of favoritism.

These requirements become particularly relevant, of course, in the case of dismissal proceedings. State regulations will provide guidelines in these matters; they must, of course, be scrupulously followed.

Design Considerations

When designing the specific instruments and procedures to be used as part of the evaluation process, educators should consider several factors. For example, how detailed should the directions be? How much choice should teachers have in what they do? What is the appropriate mix of teacher-directed and administrator-initiated activities? Designers need to address structure, choice, and applicability, among other issues.

Structure and Choice

In general, the activities required as part of an evaluation process should be tightly structured. The directions should be clear and unambiguous; teachers should know exactly what they are to do. Particularly for the required steps in the evaluation process, teachers should be asked to complete fairly specific forms and documents. For example, if the process requires teachers to submit a lesson plan, the questions to be addressed (if not the particular format) should be specified (Danielson, 1996, p. 42).

Of course, teachers should have some choice in what they submit. But structure and choice are not incompatible. For example, the evaluation process could require teachers to assemble a professional portfolio that includes a unit plan, an instructional artifact (such as an assignment sheet) from that unit, and three samples of student learning resulting from the artifact. Within these guidelines, teachers could select any unit they wanted to, and they would naturally choose one they thought demonstrated their planning skills (Danielson, 1996, p. 47).

If the directions teachers receive are vague and general, confusion and anxiety may result. For example, if the directions ask teachers merely to "provide evidence of encouraging students to think," one teacher may supply a videotape of a classroom; another, a student assignment; and still another, a letter from a parent. Further, knowing that one teacher has submitted a video, other teachers may believe that they should have done so also, and their anxiety regarding the process is likely to increase.

Similarly, an evaluation process might require teachers to submit evidence of the techniques they use for communicating with families. The written procedures might list a dozen possibilities, ranging from handouts at back-to-school night, to directions for a field trip, to a note regarding a particular student. The evaluation procedures, however, should not leave it open as to how many examples to submit; in that case, many teachers will believe that the more they submit the better, creating for themselves an unnecessary burden. Instead, the guidelines can suggest a dozen possibilities, and then ask teachers to select the three that best demonstrate the teacher's skill in the full range of situations requiring parent communication—for example, explaining the instructional program, providing information about the progress of an individual student, and outlining procedures for a class trip or other school event. Teachers need to know when they have completed the requirements of the process and should not suffer uncertainty regarding "how much is enough."

Another aspect of this question warrants mention. Different types of teacher artifacts shed light on different aspects of the evaluative criteria. And if one of the goals of the system is professional growth, then the standardization of evidence allows for coherent planning for teacher learning and growth over time. It also allows for the consistent assessment of

strengths and weaknesses across groups of teachers who may then work collaboratively on professional growth. That is, teachers might work together on improving their letters to parents, or on increasing the cognitive challenge of their instructional assignments.

Applicability

Evaluation developers should write the questions and directions in such a manner that they apply to teachers in many settings. For example, if the directions ask teachers to write a brief description of the instructional artifact they are including, the questions they are to answer should be broad enough that both 2nd grade reading teachers and high school biology teachers could apply them to their work. In other words, the questions should be generic, yet specific in nature. Here are some examples:

- "What do you hope students will learn as a result of this instructional activity?"
- "How does this activity engage students in the content?"
- "How will you determine the success of the activity in terms of student learning?"

In the design of portfolio exercises, the NBPTS has made good use of this dual principle of specificity of directions combined with wide applicability. The experience of this group suggests that clear guidelines and structure, accompanied by significant amounts of choice, provide both the best technical evaluation and the greatest professional satisfaction for the teachers completing the activities.

❧ ❧ ❧

The "how" of a teacher evaluation system is at least as important as the "what" of the system. The instruments and procedures used play an important role in both documenting the evaluative criteria and in promoting professional learning. Through the activities they are required to do as part of the system, teachers can engage in professional conversation, reflect on their practice, and analyze their own teaching. So the procedures serve not only to provide evidence of each of the evaluative criteria, but also, through their characteristics, promote professional learning.

7

The Design Process

It is one thing for a district's leadership (both teachers and administrators) to have a sense of how they want a new evaluation system to function; it is quite another undertaking to manage a process that results in such a system. This chapter addresses the challenges of translating a vision into reality, taking into account the various perspectives of everyone involved.

The process for the design of an evaluation must be as inclusive as possible. In such an important matter, there is no reason to exclude anyone who wants to be involved. An evaluation system is only as good as its acceptance by those who will use it. If the system is discredited by a significant segment of teachers, it will lose stature in the eyes of all teachers. Moreover, all educators in a school or district will have contributions to make to the design of the system; it will be a better system if the perspectives of everyone are included. Thus, schools and districts must organize the design process to ensure that all voices are heard. Last, the process of validation requires that those affected by an evaluation system judge it relevant. By engaging many educators in making decisions, designers can ensure that those judgments are made.

In addition, many teachers welcome the opportunity to engage in a process of defining good teaching. For many teachers, it may be the first opportunity for some time to engage in this important work. Moreover, they may contribute to the dialogue about how the different aspects of good teaching are manifested in different settings—how good teaching in second grade, for example, has different specific characteristics from those of excellent middle school teaching.

Step 1: Determining the Process

The first step in designing an evaluation system is to determine the general process to be followed. This process will frequently include the following elements:

• Forming an evaluation committee (which requires giving careful attention to its composition and the qualities needed in its members).
• Developing the schedule of committee meetings.
• Selecting the decision-making system to be followed.

The Evaluation Committee

Many school districts have concluded that the evaluation committee should be cochaired by representatives of both the district administration and the teachers' association. The superintendent (or an assistant superintendent for instruction) and the president of the teachers' union frequently work together to set the agendas, locate resources, and facilitate meetings. This practice of sharing the leadership of the process sends a powerful signal to all in the district, that the process has the involvement and support of everyone, and all are committed to making the process—and the resulting system—a success.

The evaluation committee should include members from different constituencies (teachers—classroom and nonclassroom—site administrators, central office administrators, association representatives, and possibly members of the board of education). Each group has its own perspective and can make its own contribution to the process. Teachers, of course, are experts in their work, and will be able to suggest changes to the evaluative criteria to make them suitable to different contexts (such as early childhood classrooms; special education classes; classes with many English-language learners; and teaching assignments, such as secondary music, in which a teacher interacts with literally hundreds of students). In addition, teachers are highly sensitive to the time demands of an evaluation process; and they will be quick to point out procedures that are overly burdensome.

Site administrators are concerned also with practical issues, particularly the competing demands on their time. They will work to ensure that the evaluation system that results from the process is one that can be managed "on the ground" in the school, given the resources at their disposal. In addition, as instructional leaders, they will want to be sure that the process yields professional learning.

Central office administrators bring a broad perspective to the process, and many of them also have extensive and valuable content expertise. Their view of education spans the entire district, and they can use their perspective to promote consistency across the district as a whole. They will also be alert to changes in state law or regulation with respect to teacher evaluation, and can ensure that the system is consistent with those mandates. Last, they will be able to oversee the implementation process that is specified, whether that involves training, production of materials, or planning for feedback sessions.

Representatives of the teachers' association will help ensure that the development process and the new evaluation system respect the rights of teachers. Moreover, associations in many areas are assuming increasing responsibility for the professional stature of their members; in those situations, they will ensure that the evaluation procedures will contribute to the teachers' professional learning and growth and, possibly, enable teachers to take more active roles in the evaluation process.

Finally, members of the board of education represent the public, and they must be satisfied that the new system reflects the type of teaching desired in the district. They will also be interested in the efficiency and utility of the evaluation system. In addition, if one member of the board of education serves on the committee, that person will develop a high level of understanding about the new system and can answer questions of other board members and serve in the role of advocate when the system is later presented to the board for approval.

Depending on the size and composition of the school district, representatives from each school (or level of school—elementary, middle, high) should be included on the committee. Schools at these different levels tend to have different cultures and different approaches to teacher collaboration, so it is important that the committee hear all perspectives. Moreover, what constitutes good teaching, or the possible ways that excellence is manifested, is somewhat different in different settings.

Qualities Needed in Members

Depending on the process the committee establishes for decision making, certain qualities will be important in committee members. These might include their level of interest, their open-mindedness, and their communication skills, among other qualities.

Interest. Not everyone is interested in the challenges presented by designing a new system for teacher evaluation. The work is difficult and requires the sustained attention of everyone involved, so it is important for committee members to bring enthusiasm to the task. Many educators are intensely interested in professional learning; the idea that an evaluation system can encourage such learning may be new to some people, but is a concept they are keen to explore.

Commitment to the Project. Teacher evaluation is a very important aspect of the culture of a school or district; those involved in the design process must be committed to its success. There is no place in a committee process for individuals who are looking for ways to undermine the effort, who want the project to fail. Committee members should recognize that they are to be part of designing a system that they themselves would want to use.

Willingness to Participate. Discussions at committee meetings, while they will be clearly focused, will be spirited at times. If committee members sit back and let the discussion go on around them, their school, or level, or their own particular view, will not be adequately represented. Participation from every committee member is essential; otherwise a few individuals can dominate both the discussion and the committee's decisions.

Open-mindedness. Members of the committee must be willing to listen carefully to diverse viewpoints before arriving at a conclusion. They must be willing to abandon a position when confronted with new information or a new perspective that causes them to change their mind. These alternate points of view may come from either members of the committee or from colleagues at the school site.

Leadership. Membership on an evaluation committee is not a suitable role for a retiring or passive individual. The work is formidable, and the decisions are difficult. The explanations of the committee's work to one's colleagues may, at times, be subjected to challenge. Committee members must be able to explain the committee's thinking and provide the rationale for recommendations without becoming defensive.

Communication Skills. An important role for committee members is to serve as a liaison between the committee and the staff of each school. An important part of this function may be to provide reports of committee activities to colleagues at the school site. In addition, committee members should be able to listen carefully to the views of their colleagues and to convey these views to the full committee.

The Schedule of Meetings

Regular meetings of the evaluation committee are essential to allow the work to move forward. How frequently should they be held? Will they be held during the day or after school hours? One approach is to hold the meetings of the evaluation committee monthly (say, on the second Tuesday of each month) for the equivalent of a half day or a full day. This schedule provides for a meeting of sufficient duration that members may hold substantive discussions. It also allows work to proceed between meetings, for example, for minutes to be written and circulated to members of the committee for presentation to other staff members. Depending on the composition of the committee and the number of substitute teachers required to permit classroom teachers to attend during school hours, the meetings might have to be held in the late afternoon and evening. If this is the case, the committee will require sustenance, either with members providing refreshments, or with a meal brought in.

The Decision-making Process to Be Followed

The group should designate one person as the facilitator of the committee process. Some responsibilities of the facilitator are as follows:

• Preparing the agendas and materials for the committee to consider.
• Arranging for substitute teachers, if needed.
• Preparing the meeting room and securing refreshments.
• Contacting consultants (if these are used) and preparing them for their work with the group.
• Collecting comments from the entire staff (when these are requested) and summarizing them for the committee's review.
• Facilitating the actual meetings.

The process used should include the opportunity for all staff to be informed of the progress of the committee and to contribute to the

committee's deliberations. Above all, no one should feel that the new teacher evaluation process was developed by a secretive, remote process that was closed to outsiders. If the size of the district does not permit every school to be represented on the committee, then the committee should develop procedures that permit teachers and administrators from those schools to be kept abreast of the committee's work and to have opportunities to contribute their ideas.

One possible approach to this challenge is to develop a formal schedule for discussing the committee's work:

• The facilitator would summarize all committee work shortly following the meeting (say, within three days.) If meetings are held on the second Tuesday of each month, for example, the summaries would be completed by the second Friday of the month.
• Then, each committee member, at a regularly scheduled faculty meeting the following week (sometime during the third week), would make a brief presentation to the full faculty of the committee's latest work and circulate any materials that resulted from the meeting (for example, recommendations about differentiated evaluation procedures for different types of teachers).
• The committee member conducts a brief discussion with the full faculty and clarifies any rationale for the committee's recommendations.
• The faculty then has a week to react to the recommendations, giving them to the committee member by the end of the fourth week of the month.
• The committee member forwards these comments to the facilitator (including any

interpretations, if such are needed), who summarizes the comments from every school in time for the committee to consider them at its next meeting, on the second Tuesday of the next month.

For those schools without a representative on the committee, the building principal can serve in the role of conducting this process with the faculty.

Another possible approach to developing a new teacher evaluation process is to create the committee in the late spring, before the long summer vacation. Then, the committee could schedule a two- or three-day extended meeting (compensated, if possible) during the summer, during which they take a hard look at the total project and formulate tentative recommendations on all the major components of the system. In this case, then, the meetings during the school year can be shorter, less frequent, and devoted to making revisions to the system based on the reaction and feedback of teachers to drafts produced by the committee.

Figure 7.1 outlines a possible process for one year's work on the evaluation system.

Step 2: Using the Process, Determining the General Procedures (the "How")

There is no single sequence in which to proceed in the design of an evaluation system, and logic would suggest that the committee turn its attention to the "what" before it addresses the "how." Many educators, however, find that the procedural issues involved (that is, who does what, and when) are more immediately engaging than the more cerebral issues involved in deciding the evaluative criteria. So, although

the recommendations about procedures are not necessarily the logical place to begin, they are frequently the developmental place to start.

The general procedures for an evaluation system include attention to the following issues:

- Differentiated procedures for different groups of teachers.
- Time lines for evaluation activities.
- Different types of evaluation activities.
- Personnel involved in evaluation.
- Due process and equity.

See Chapter 6 for a discussion of these issues.

On the question of evaluation activities, the committee should answer the following question: "What types of activities should teachers engage in as part of the evaluation process?" If the committee has determined that different groups of teachers (for example, tenured and nontenured) should engage in different types of activities, through a differentiated approach, then they will have to decide which activities are used by whom, and at what stage.

See Chapter 5 for a discussion of the following activities:

- Classroom observation.
- Teacher self-assessment.
- Planning documents—unit plans, individual lesson plan.
- Teaching artifacts, such as assignments, worksheets, project directions.
- Samples of student work, or other evidence of student learning.
- Parent and community communications.
- Logs of professional development activities, school or district projects.
- Student and parent surveys.

The evaluation committee might decide that the formal evaluation process will include some

	FIGURE 7.1		
	Teacher Evaluation Design Process		
Date	**School Faculties**	**Evaluation Committee**	**District Administration**
Month 1		Determine the general decision-making procedure to be followed	
Month 2		Consider different options for a general process (differentiation, general time lines, different procedures, personnel to be involved); outline options and recommendations	
Month 3	Review committee recommendations for the general process to be followed, consider options, make suggestions	Consider suggestions from school faculties and district administration; make final determination	Review committee recommendations for the general process to be followed, consider options, make suggestions
Month 4		Draft the "what" (the evaluative criteria, the levels of performance, their relative weights, and the questions related to standards of performance)	
Month 5	Review committee recommendations for the "what," consider options, make suggestions	Revise the "what" based on suggestions from school faculties and district administrators	Review committee recommendations for the "what," consider options, make suggestions
Month 6	Review committee recommendations for instruments and procedures, consider options, make suggestions	Draft the detailed instruments and procedures, considering the evaluative criteria and the general procedures already determined	Review committee recommendations for instruments and procedures, consider options, make suggestions

(continued)

69

		FIGURE 7.1 (continued)	
Date	**School Faculties**	**Evaluation Committee**	**District Administration**
Month 7		Revise the detailed instruments and procedures based on suggestions from the school faculties and district administrators	Present a preliminary report to the board of education; respond to questions; solicit suggestions
		As necessary, make revisions to the system based on suggestions from the board of education	
Month 8	Review committee recommendations regarding a plan for implementation, consider options, make suggestions	Draft the plan for implementation of the new system	Review committee recommendations regarding a plan for implementation, consider options, make suggestions
Month 9		Revise the implementation plan based on suggestions from the school faculties and district administration	
Month 10	Review committee recommendations concerning training for evaluators and orientation for teachers, consider options, make suggestions	Design the training program for evaluators and orientation plan for teachers	Review committee recommendations concerning training for evaluators and orientation for teachers, consider options, make suggestions
Month 11		Finalize all plans; submit to the district administration for presentation to the board of education	Present new evaluation system to the board of education for approval

combination of the activities listed, the specific activities depending on the particular evaluative criteria adopted. In addition, many of these are activities that promote professional learning. That is, they require thoughtful reflection about teaching and, therefore, encourage teachers to examine their practice; such reflection produces professional growth.

In addition, if the committee has adopted an evaluation system involving formal evaluation only every two, three, or four years, the committee might decide that a different series of activities could be used in the other years. That is, they might decide that activities centered on self-directed professional growth should be required in the nonformal evaluation years, and could include self-assessment, formulation of growth goals, and participation in study groups.

The evaluation committee may summarize its planning for the entire process (the activities, time lines, and personnel) by completing a chart such as that displayed in Figure 7.2 (p. 72). This chart assumes a multiyear evaluation cycle for nonprobationary teachers and the possibility of differentiated procedures for probationary and nonprobationary teachers. It also assumes that the evaluation year runs from August through June rather than, for example, March through March. These all represent decisions that the committee would make regarding evaluation procedures.

Step 3: Using the Process, Determine the Evaluative Criteria (the "What")

The evaluative criteria are at the heart of any evaluation process. The criteria, taken together, define teaching in the district, and reflect the district's educational philosophy.

They can be organized, as described in Chapter 4 ("The Evaluative Criteria, or the 'What'"), either as "inputs"—that is, descriptions of the tasks of teaching—or as "outputs"—typically some measure of student learning, or some combination of the two.

Using the process, the evaluation committee decides the evaluative criteria, on at least a preliminary basis. (The committee may revise the criteria later in the process, when they design the detailed instruments and procedures.) The "what" of the evaluation includes the following:

• The evaluative criteria, including the relative weights of each.
• Descriptions of levels of performance on each criterion.
• General recommendations regarding the expectations for performance of teachers at different stages in their careers.

Some evaluation systems (for example, the one in Coventry, Rhode Island) provide for a graduated approach to evaluation for probationary teachers. For example, the district evaluates first-year teachers on only 7 of the 22 components of *Enhancing Professional Practice: A Framework for Teaching* (Danielson, 1996); and another 5 components are added in the second year. It is not until the third year of teaching that teachers must demonstrate skill in all 22 components of the framework.

Step 4: Using the Process, Determine the Detailed Instruments and Procedures

Instruments and procedures refer to the actual forms and guidelines used in the evaluation

		Nonprobationary Teacher Activities	
Month	**Probationary Teacher Activities**	**Formal Evaluation Years**	**Self-Directed Professional Growth Years**
August		(Throughout the year) Teacher collects evidence of student learning and professional activities	Teacher conducts self-assessment
September	Administrator conducts the first formal observation	Teacher and administrator conduct initial conference	Teacher and principal hold goal-setting conference
October			Teacher forms study group; formulates growth plan
November		Administrator conducts first formal observation	Study groups meet monthly; implement growth plans
December	Administrator conducts the second formal observation		
January		Administrator conducts second formal observation	
February			
March	Administrator completes evaluation; holds conference with teacher	Teacher and administrator hold conference to examine teacher artifacts	
April			Teachers conduct self-assessment and reflect on the professional growth process
May		Administrator completes evaluation, holds conference with teacher	
June			

FIGURE 7.2
A Plan for Evaluation

process. They would include such things as the format for unit or lesson plans, the forms used during classroom observations, directions and procedures for analyzing student work, and the specific questions used in an interview or conference.

The instruments and procedures used will depend on the evaluative criteria. In addition, the instruments should satisfy certain criteria. As described in Chapter 6, they should

- Taken together, serve to document all the criteria, and provide the opportunity for teachers to demonstrate performance at the highest level.
- Represent, to the extent possible, a "natural harvest" of teachers' work, rather than consisting of extra work that teachers must do solely for the evaluation process.
- Constitute valuable professional development by, for example, encouraging self-assessment and reflection on practice.
- Consist of reasonable workloads for individuals, both teachers and administrators.
- Contain clear and unambiguous directions and questions.
- Apply to the full range of teaching contexts.
- Include an appropriate degree of choice for teachers.

Members of the evaluation committee may discover, in the development of the detailed instruments and procedures, that they cannot design assessments for some of the evaluative criteria. For example, they may have identified "teacher belief in the innate potential of each student" as an evaluative criterion. But what would count as evidence of such a belief? It is impossible to assess the content of a person's

mind directly. The committee must then determine whether to (1) determine what would count as reasonable indicators of the criteria in question, (2) revisit the criteria (the "what") and revise them so they can be assessed directly, or (3) accept that some aspects of performance cannot be assessed in a systematic manner.

Step 5: Using the Process, Determine the Plan for Implementation

The committee may implement a new process for teacher evaluation in several different ways. If the committee has faithfully followed its own development process and all staff have had an opportunity to contribute to the new system, it should be fairly clear how responsive the staff is likely to be to the new approach.

One option, of course, is for all staff to begin using the new approach at the outset. Many schools and districts, however, recognize that any new evaluation system is bound to be imperfect; and many schools undergo "shake-down cruises" to correct initial difficulties. They decide to adopt a plan to phase in the new system. The following are options for phasing in:

- Volunteers from across the district use the new system and provide feedback.
- All the teachers in a sample of schools use the new system.
- The system is introduced with probationary teachers only.
- The system is used at first with a small, but nonvoluntary, subset of the teachers in the school or district, such as those whose name begins with A–E.

Of course, the school board may have already determined a timetable for implementation. If that is the case, teachers and administrators will be obliged to follow it. Even in this case, however, many boards are open to a revision in the schedule if there are compelling reasons for it.

Step 6: Designing the Training Program for Evaluators

Teachers must have the benefit of evaluators who can make consistent judgments; a teacher's performance appraisal should not depend on the identity of the evaluator. The goal, therefore, of the assessor training program is to produce trained assessors who can make reliable judgments based on evidence.

The process of evaluating teaching is a complex cognitive task, with many opportunities for discussion and debate. As Figure 7.3 shows, the process begins with data collection. In any given observation, or in any portfolio, there is a mass of data; part of the skill of the evaluator is to determine which of the "data points" are relevant to each of the evaluative criteria. There are choices to be made, of course. For example, if a video of a classroom lesson shows confusion around the pencil sharpener, is this evidence for the criterion about classroom routines and procedures, or the one on standards of conduct, or both? Is all the evidence collected for a given criterion representative of the whole, and not skewed one way or another? For example, does it include only negative evidence?

Next, the evaluator must take all the evidence for a criterion and impose an interpretation on it. Frequently, more than one interpretation is possible, which is why it is important for teachers and administrators to discuss the evidence together. For example, an administrator might observe a teacher decline to answer a student's question, and conclude from the episode that the teacher's content knowledge was weak. On the other hand, the teacher might have deliberately chosen to not answer the student's question because the teacher wanted to challenge the student to find the answer independently. It might have been a pedagogical decision that the evaluator confused for a lack of content knowledge.

After the evidence for the criterion has been collected and interpreted, the assessor must use it to make a judgment against the descriptions of levels of performance for the criterion. If the levels appear as a four-point scale, the evaluator must determine which point of the scale is best represented by the evidence, as interpreted. Then the evaluator must assemble the judgments for all the criteria to determine an overall rating on total teacher performance.

The evaluator training program, therefore, should equip administrators or other evaluators for this complex task. The training should be carefully designed; haphazard discussion, or a superficial review of the forms, is completely inadequate. At a minimum, future evaluators should spend two days in structured activities and dialogue around the following topics:

• The evaluative criteria and the ways in which they may be manifested in different settings.
• The dangers of personal bias in observing and analyzing teaching.
• The nature of evidence and how it is distinguished from personal opinion.
• Evaluation of teacher performance (using videotapes of lessons and other evidence, such

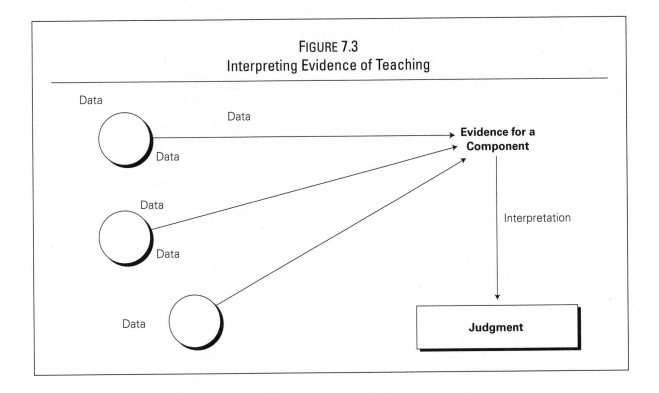

FIGURE 7.3
Interpreting Evidence of Teaching

as instructional artifacts, lesson plans, and parent communication) against the evaluative criteria, with an emphasis on consistency of judgment from one assessor to another.

• The use of district-approved forms and instruments.

• The structure of the evaluation system, with an emphasis on the particular responsibilities (as specified in the time lines) for evaluators.

Figure 7.4 (pp. 76–77) shows a possible outline for a two-day evaluator training program.

Ideally, newly trained evaluators should have the opportunity to practice their observation and judgment skills before using them with teachers when it "counts." If it can be arranged, they should practice, in pairs, observing in classrooms and comparing their

impressions. Not all teachers, of course, will volunteer to being observed by a pair of administrators so the administrators can improve their skills. Some will be happy to, particularly if they understand that the "evaluation" conducted is for administrator practice only and cannot be used against them.

Most participants in an assessor training program find it to be a highly rewarding professional experience, one in which they engage in significant dialogue and achieve an enhanced understanding of teaching expertise. Most people report that their understanding of good instruction improves and that they become more discerning in their own instructional decisions.

In addition to a training program for evaluators, a well-designed approach to implementation of an evaluation system will include

| | FIGURE 7.4 | |
| | Observation Skills Workshop | |
Time	Activity	Summary
Day 1		
15 minutes	Introduction; overview of workshop	Review of housekeeping details, schedule, agenda. Introductions; sharing of expectations
30 minutes	Review of evaluation procedures, timelines	This is conducted by local officials, reviewing the procedures that will be followed
30 minutes	Bias exercise	Through a series of exercises, participants recognize the role of bias in making professional judgments, and identify their own biases
15 minutes	The nature of evidence, interpretation, judgment	Trainer reviews the relationships among data points, selection of evidence, interpretation, and judgment in assessment
60 minutes	Examples of performance	Participants sort vignettes according to domains, components, and levels of performance
30 minutes	Note-taking procedures	Participants share techniques they have found successful for note-taking during classroom observation; trainer reviews the distinction between observed behavior and value-laden descriptions
Lunch		
45 minutes	Assessing Domain 1	Participants review planning documents, and evaluate performance using the descriptions of performance
45 minutes	Collecting evidence; assessing performance in Domain 2	Participants watch videotapes; collect evidence, and assess performance for the components in Domain 2. Benchmark performances are used to establish the standards; then participants evaluate performance independently. Trainer leads a discussion in which participants share their evidence and resolve differences
45 minutes	Collecting evidence; assessing performance in Domain 3	Participants watch videotapes; collect evidence, and assess performance for the components in Domain 3. Benchmark performances are used to establish the standards; then participants evaluate performance independently. Trainer leads a discussion in which participants share their evidence and resolve differences
30 minutes	Conducting reflective conversations	Trainer presents the skills of reflective conversation; participants practice these skills in a role-play exercise

Time	Activity	Summary
FIGURE 7.4 (continued)		
Day 2		
90 minutes	A complete evaluation	Participants review all materials for a lesson, including planning documents, samples of student work; watch videotape of lesson, take notes, and assess performance in Domains 1, 2, and 3; write summary statements
30 minutes	Review of results of evaluation; share assessments; arrive at consensus	Trainer invites participants to share evidence and assessments; presents "answers" as needed. Participants share summaries of the lesson
30 minutes	Evaluating performance in Domain 4	Participants review artifacts for documenting performance in Domain 4; they evaluate them against the descriptions of levels of performance; discuss their interpretations
Lunch		
150 minutes	Proficiency exercise	Participants complete evaluation, independently, with all the materials needed to assess performance in all the domains
30 minutes	Review proficiency exercise	Participants review their performance on the proficiency exercise against the juried scores; discuss discrepancies and determine possible needs for additional experience

Note: For a description of the domains, see Figure 3.1, "Components of Professional Practice," p. 23.

adequate orientation for teachers who will be evaluated using the new system. This can include many of the same elements contained in the training program for evaluators, but with an emphasis on understanding and demonstrating the evaluative criteria, rather than in assessing them.

☛ ☛ ☛

In the design of the evaluation system, the evaluation committee merges the principles of quality assurance and professional growth and translates this new entity into reality. By using an inclusive process; by considering the different needs and skills of teachers at different stages in their careers; by developing procedures that maximize self-assessment, reflection, and professional conversation, schools and districts can make the most of teacher evaluation. Naturally, it is a time-consuming challenge—one that requires an investment of mental energy. But the overwhelming feedback from those school districts that have embarked on such a project is that it is well worth the commitment required.

Preamble to Chapters 8–10:
The Structural Framework for Designing the Evaluation System

hapters 1–7 have provided the background to help you understand and justify the need for and the shape of new designs for teacher evaluation systems. We are proposing that teacher evaluation be based on a *research-based set of teaching standards*. Teacher evaluation should be built around a range of sources of data and information, allowing teachers to demonstrate their mastery of the standards. In addition, teacher evaluation should provide opportunities for teachers at different stages to be involved in different processes and activities. Finally, teacher evaluation should be heavily focused on the *formative* aspects of evaluation, using staff-directed activities for the purpose of promoting professional learning.

To accomplish these desired outcomes, the majority of school districts that are redesigning their evaluation program use a basic three-track model as their framework. Figure 8.1 (p. 79) provides an example of the three-track model used in the East Grand Rapids, Michigan, School District.

This overview of the proposed evaluation program will serve as the organizational framework for Chapter 8 (Track I—Initial Staff Development, or the Beginning Teacher Program Track), Chapter 9 (Track II—The Professional Development Track), and Chapter 10 (Track III—The Teacher Assistance Track). In addition, some state departments of education have been engaged in the redesign of their systems for teacher evaluation. For example, Delaware plans to pilot a new system in September 2000, with full implementation in September 2001. This new system is based on the ASCD book *Enhancing Professional Practice: A Framework for Teaching* (Danielson, 1996) and includes provision for three tracks: novice teachers, experienced teachers, and teachers needing intensive assistance. Figure 8.1a (p. 80) summarizes its provisions.

FIGURE 8.1
Overview of Teacher Evaluation Program

Standards for Effective Teaching

I.	Classroom Environment	IV.	Assessment
II.	Preparation and Planning	V.	Communication and Professional Responsibilities
III.	Instruction		

Plan I Initial Staff Development	Plan II Professional Growth	Plan III Specific Staff Development
Who: • Teachers with less than four years teaching experience • Teachers who have not taught previously in Michigan • Michigan tenured teachers	**Who:** • Tenured teachers who are demonstrating the Standards for Effective Teaching	**Who:** • Teachers in need of specific professional guidance in identified area(s) of the Standards for Effective Teaching
Purpose: • To ensure that Standards for Effective Teaching are understood, accepted, and demonstrated • To provide support in implementing the Standards • To provide accountability for decisions to continue employment	**Purpose:** • To enhance professional growth • To improve student achievement • To provide feedback on professional issues • To focus on school improvement initiatives	**Purpose:** • To give a tenured teacher the opportunity to seek assistance in any Standard • To provide a more structured process for a tenured teacher who may benefit from more support • To provide due process for disciplinary action

What:
• For observations and evaluation of performance
• Portfolio
• Reflection
• Mentor
	What:
	• Informal observations to assess Standards
	• Develop and implement Professional Growth Plan
		What:
		• Three Phases
		  1. Awareness Phase
		  2. Assistance Phase
		  3. Disciplinary Phase

Method: • Classroom observation with feedback • Review of portfolio • Discussion of professional practices • Mentor support	**Method:** • Ongoing informal discussion of teacher performance • Teacher teams/individual teacher develop a Professional Growth Plan • Collaboration between teacher teams/teacher and administrator • Establish indicators of progress • Administrative support of teacher teams/teacher • Feedback to teacher teams/teacher	**Method:** • Observation and feedback focused specifically on identified area(s) of needed improvement

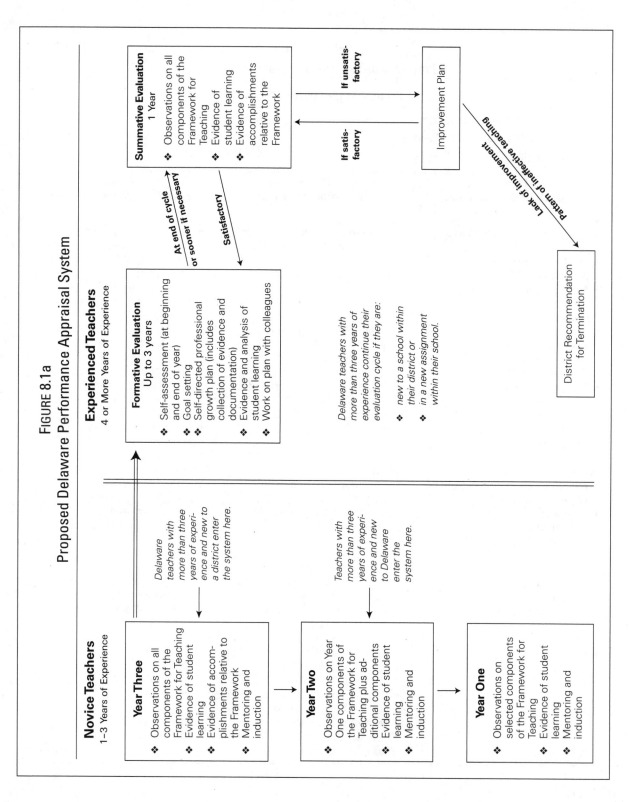

FIGURE 8.1a
Proposed Delaware Performance Appraisal System

8

Track I—The Beginning Teacher Program

The primary purpose of Track I is to generate usable and reliable data that will support making a decision to retain a probationary teacher and eventually move her to a tenured or continuing contract position. The procedures, processes, and relationships established and supported within Track I should also help new staff develop professionally and personally, promote an environment that will encourage teachers and administrators to understand the importance and usefulness of evaluation, and support the practice of reflection and professional learning. These latter purposes take on added importance if the district does not already have in place quality induction and mentoring programs.

Coordination with Induction and Mentoring

If an induction program is in place and the district assigns mentors to new teachers, then the evaluation committee should ensure that the Track I evaluation program acknowledges and supports existing induction and mentoring programs. The district should review and coordinate all three programs—induction, mentoring, and evaluation—to prevent overlapping

responsibilities or work. Although Track I includes a summative evaluation component separate from the other two programs, all other functions of these programs are complementary, and the designs of all three programs should reflect this idea.

Who Is Involved and for How Long?

Track I is designed for all teachers new to the school district. This would automatically include all teachers who are just starting their teaching careers. Each state or local district usually has its own labels for this group (e.g., probationary teachers, nontenured teachers, initial licensure teachers). Involvement in this track would be determined by the length of the required probationary period determined by state statutes (generally between two and four years). Each district must also determine how it will handle newly hired experienced teachers. In most states, tenured teachers moving from one district to another or from another state lose their tenure. Consequently, they join the district as nontenured teachers. Most schools require all newly hired veterans to go through the beginning teacher programs for at least the first two years. This required involvement, local educators believe, helps veterans learn more quickly and deeply the values and expectations of the district. If the full beginning-teacher program encompasses four years, then the system should include options allowing veterans who have demonstrated competency in meeting the district teaching standards to move to the professional growth track (Track II) ahead of schedule.

As part of an increasing commitment to ensure teacher accountability, many states have been extending the length of the probationary period for nontenured teachers. Local districts must decide how these extended probationary periods will affect the way that they structure their evaluation system and when they establish major decision points. Many districts decide that the end of the second year of probationary status is a critical time for decision making. If the district has established a clear set of teaching standards and has incorporated valid and reliable means for collecting evidence of progress toward meeting the standards, then the district should be able to make serious retention decisions.

Many districts believe it is unfair to a new teacher and inefficient for the district to retain beginning teachers to the end of their probationary period and then not award tenure. For this reason, districts are making distinctions between the required activities in the beginning track for the first two years and what is required in the remaining years of the state-mandated probationary status. For example, districts will decrease the number of required observations, drop any required collections of teacher-designed materials or student work samples, and alter such supplementary activities as journal writing, portfolio development, and participation in mentoring programs. In addition, districts are encouraging new

teachers in the latter years of probation to become involved in activities that are more a part of Track II, to ease the transition into these more self-directed programs. Such transitional activities also serve to lighten the workloads on supervisors by allowing them to focus much of their time and energy on the crucial first two years.

Adequate Time and Effort

To meet the range of expectations for Track I, the district must make a serious commitment of time and resources to this program. The experience of districts with evaluation systems perceived as effective suggests that supervisors or their designees should spend about 10–14 hours of contact time with each new teacher per year. This time would decrease in the later years in those states or districts that have an extended probationary experience (three or more years). This "contact time" includes time for the following:

- Conferences.
- Observations.
- Supervisor-teacher interactions generated by alternative data-collection activities.
- The reading of journals or portfolios.
- Informal visits and conversations.

This time would be over and above any time the new teacher spends in induction activities or attending mandatory staff development activities. These guidelines make serious time demands on administrative staff. New procedures in working with tenured, competent staff, however, should free some time; and the option of involving more people than just the principal in the evaluation process would also decrease the time demands. As many effective principals and other school leaders will testify, however, there is no more important responsibility for school administrators than working with new staff.

Multiple Participants

Whenever possible, schools and districts should allow—or require—other staff to participate in working with nontenured staff. In dealing with issues of renewal or retention, however, districts usually require administrators to make the summative decisions. This demands that administrators play the dominant role in data collection. Even in this case, a growing number of districts and states are using, encouraging, or requiring forms of peer appraisal and review (PAR) and peer coaching processes for making summative judgments. For example, the new Teacher Peer Review and Assistance program in California provides financial incentives for local districts to involve teaching staff in the review of their colleagues. This is not yet a widespread initiative; but recommended or mandated teacher involvement in this process may become a trend sooner than we might have expected. Obviously, a local district must deal with any state mandates or state incentive programs regarding peer involvement as it designs new evaluation procedures.

Other options that are available to ease the time demands on any one principal include using assistant principals, department heads, content supervisors, district or building staff development specialists, and central office personnel. The use of other staff may be warranted by the number of new teachers entering a particular school in any given year. Districts should use such alternate supervisors to relieve the pressure on a principal who is faced with an unusual or unexpected number of new staff; in addition, alternate supervisory staff can add important and different perspectives to the evaluation process. No one combination of involved staff is better than another. A good guideline would be that the more knowledgeable alternate supervisors or staff members are about the new teacher's particular context, the more useful their input and involvement.

Primary Sources of Data

Chapter 5 described sources of information and their possible use and usefulness in local teacher evaluation systems. Given the specific purposes of the Track I beginning teacher program, most schools seem to prefer certain sources in their design process. In this chapter, for convenience, we refer to a hypothetical district that has adopted the standards in Danielson's 1996 book *Enhancing Professional Practice: A Framework for Teaching,* as the focus of its teacher evaluation system. The examples of forms and instrumentation are taken from schools that are currently using this framework. Based on our reviews of best practices, we believe that classroom observations and collections of teacher artifacts—and the accompanying directions and instrumentation described in this chapter—should be required activities within Track I. Additional sources of data, including journals, portfolios, and mentoring programs, could be optional sources.

Structured Classroom Observations

Classroom observation remains the most practical activity for collecting formal data about teacher performance. The quality of observations and the ways supervisors collect and share data with teachers are major factors in the success and effectiveness of teacher evaluation systems. We use the term *structured observations* purposefully. A structured or formal observation should be based on the classic clinical supervision model. It provides a powerful training activity while also giving the observer the most accurate and reliable picture of what is and has occurred. Most new systems require somewhere between two and six formal observations during the school year. The number will generally be determined on the basis of supervisor time and the number of other experiences required of the nontenured teachers.

A formal or structured observation includes a pre-conference, the observation, and a post-conference.

Pre-conference with the Teacher. The reliability and usefulness of classroom observation is directly related to the amount and type of information supervisors have *before* the observation. This is especially true in the model proposed here because the supervisor and teacher should be focusing their energy on a specific set of teaching standards. To ensure a focus on district standards, many schools have developed pre-conference forms completed by the teacher and brought to the conference. If time requirements are extensive for new teachers, supervisors may not require teachers to complete the form before the conference but still use it as the guide for the conference. Figure 8.2* provides an example of such a document as used in the Addison School District #4, in Addison, Illinois. Most questions on the form are tied to

one of the components in the Danielson (1996) framework. The conversation generated by this document directs the pre-conference and sets the stage for the observation. Most districts that use this type of structuring activity find it helpful.

The Observation. The clinical supervision model, as it was originally conceived, was a formative evaluation experience that asked the observer to be a collector of descriptive data on predetermined aspects of the teacher's performance. This view has been compromised over the years by the use of clinical supervision as a summative evaluation activity. The requirements for nontenured teacher evaluation make summative judgments based on observation necessary. In that respect, the recommended observational activity is an adaptation of clinical supervision. Remember that the observation is *not* the evaluation. Unfortunately, many districts and their staffs equate observation and evaluation. Observation is a source of data for use in collecting evidence and for use as a focus for professional discussion and reflection on teaching and learning. It is one of the information-gathering activities available to the supervisor that, when taken together, help inform professional judgment. To make the observation as reliable as possible, districts should train supervisors or other observers in observation and conferencing skills. Wherever possible, the district should link this training to the standards for teaching the district adopted. Chapter 7 provides more details about the training requirements for these new evaluation programs.

Requiring a specific number of formal observations does not prevent the evaluator from using informal observations (unannounced observations, walk-throughs, drop-ins).

---

*Note that Figures 8.1 and 8.1a are in the Preamble to Chapters 8–10.

FIGURE 8.2
Pre-observation Form

Addison School District 4
Pretenured Teacher

Name _____ School/Administrator _____

Date of Preconference _____ Date/Time of Observation _____

Grade Level/Curriculum Area Observed _____

1. Briefly describe the students in this class, including those with special needs. (Component 1b)	6. How do you plan to engage students in the content? What will you do? What will the students do?
2. What are the goals for the lesson? What do you want the students to learn? (Component 1c)	7. What difficulties do students typically experience in this area, and how do you plan to anticipate these difficulties? (Component 1a)
3. Why are these goals suitable for this group of students? (Component 1c)	8. What instructional materials or other resources, if any will you use? (Attach sample materials you will be using in the lesson.) (Component 1d)
4. How do these goals support the district's curriculum, state frameworks, and the content standards?	9. How do you plan to assess student achievement of the goals? What procedures will you use? (Attach any tests or performance tasks, with rubrics or scoring guides.) (Component 1f)
5. How do these goals relate to broader curriculum goals in the discipline as a whole or in other disciplines? (Component 1c)	10. How do you plan to use the results of the assessment?

Teacher comments pertaining to observation setting. List any items you might want to call to the attention of the Administrator.

Observational Focus:

Note: Components 1a–1f are described in Figure 3.1 (p. 23).

Contrary to popular belief, unannounced visits do not provide more accurate pictures of teaching than do announced visits. They are most useful as opportunities to see specific activities such as the start of class, certain transition times, student demonstrations, or other special events. Most districts will add a proviso to the written description of Track I that indicates that other forms of observation may occur and may be considered a part of the evaluation process.

A major tenet of successful observation is that the accuracy and usefulness of classroom observation is directly related to the supervisor's use of a narrow focus of observation. Using the standards for performance in Danielson's (1996) framework helps provide this needed focus. Because of its recognized efficiency and widespread acceptance by teachers, observation becomes a primary source of evidence in holding a teacher's performance up against the standards. To advance the reliability of this process, many districts are using some form of observation guide to focus the attention of the observer and to remind the teacher of what is expected. Figure 8.3 shows an observation guide used by many districts that have adopted Danielson's framework as their teaching standards. Figure 8.3 is an observation guide for Domains 2 and 3. If schools or districts decide to use an observation guide, they should provide training on the use of the guide for all who will be serving as observers.

The Post-observation Conference. The conference following the observation is directed specifically at what happened during the observation. As with the pre-observation conference, there can be a one- to three-day time period between the conference and the observation. If the evaluator uses an observation guide, the comments provided by the observer on the guide serve as the focus of the conversation. To add to the usefulness of the post-conference, observers should confine their comments on structured observation guides or any other form of written comments to descriptions and questions, rather than judgments. Post-conferences are a time for reflection,

review, constructive feedback, and reinforcement. The final evaluative conference that occurs after a series of observations and other activities within the required procedures is the appropriate time for documenting evidence that leads to a summative evaluation.

To support the use of the post-conference as a time for reflection and review, many districts are using a post-observation reflection form for the teacher to use. The teacher brings the completed form to the conference and shares it with the observer. Figure 8.4 shows such a form being used in the Addison School District. As with the preconference form, the components refer to elements of Danielson's (1996) frameworks.

Extended-Duration Observation. Some districts are adding a different dimension to their observation requirements by either mandating or strongly recommending that at least one of the observations for new teachers during year one or two be of extended duration. New views of teaching, such as strategies suggested for teaching for understanding, are promoting more engaged learning with more of an emphasis on multitask activities. These new ideas place more complex demands on the planning process. Consequently, we are suggesting that before a school or district places any new elementary teacher on a continuing contract (tenure), an evaluator should observe the teacher at least once for an entire day. Elementary schoolteachers face complex demands during the school day: teaching four or five different content areas in a single day, experiencing the erosion of allocated time periods because of pullout programs, having increased numbers of special needs students, and holding higher expectations for student learning. It is becoming impossible to determine—during a

---

FIGURE 8.3
Classroom Observation Record

Name_____School_____

Grade Level_____Subject_____School Year _____

Observer Name _____Position_____

Component 2a: Creating an Environment of Respect and Rapport	Component 3a: Communicating Clearly and Accurately
Component 2b: Establishing a Culture for Learning	Component 3b: Using Questioning and Discussion Techniques
Component 2c: Managing Classroom Procedures	Component 3c: Engaging Students in Learning
Component 2d: Managing Student Behavior	Component 3d: Providing Feedback to Students
Component 2e: Organizing Physical Space	Component 3e: Demonstrating Flexibility and Responsiveness

Source: Danielson, C. (1996). *Enhancing professional practice: A framework for teaching.* Alexandria, VA: Association for Supervision and Curriculum Development.

---

one-hour observation—a teacher's ability to plan and implement effective teaching.

Because administrative personnel lack the necessary time to devote to extended observations, most districts are finding the all-day recommendation to be excessive. But many districts are including the extended-duration observation in their requirements and are using two- to three-hour observations as the definition. Evaluation committees in middle school and high school are using the same rationale. Expectations for secondary school classrooms

FIGURE 8.4
Observation Reflection Form

Addison School District 4
Pretenured Teacher

Name _____ School_____

Grade/Subject_____

Observation Date_____ Time _____

Post Conference Date_____ Time _____

1. As I reflect on the lesson, to what extent were students productively engaged? (Component 4a, 1e, 3c)

2. Did the students learn what I intended? Were my instructional goals met? How do I know? (Components 1f and 4a)

3. Did I alter my goals or instructional plan as I taught the lesson? If so, why? (Component 1e and 3e)

4. If I had the opportunity to teach this lesson again to this same group of students, what would I do differently? Why? (Component 4a)

5. Provide several samples of student work on this assignment. This work should reflect the full range of student ability in your class and include feedback you provide to students on their papers.

Teacher's signature/date _____

Administrator's signature/date_____

This form will be filed at the school level.

are also raising the bar on levels of student engagement. Classroom instruction that encourages more active, authentic teaching, when combined with reform initiatives dealing with alternative scheduling, has altered the basic use of time in many classrooms. For new teachers in middle, junior, and senior high schools, we recommend that evaluation committees define an observation of extended duration as observing the teacher during the same period over three consecutive days. This form of observation provides good evidence of the teacher's ability to link days and events and to display a fuller range of instructional and assessment strategies than is possible in a single class period. Districts should consider observations of an extended duration as a part of the beginning teacher program. Figure 8.5 (p. 90) shows how the East Grand Rapids School District in Michigan incorporates observation as part of their Track I program.

Artifact Collection or Document Analysis

Another activity that many districts are using as a required part of beginning teacher evaluation programs is artifact collection or document analysis. It has been well documented that the majority of students in preK–12 classrooms spend as much, if not more, time interacting with the "stuff" of teaching than they do being directly instructed by the teacher. As student involvement with technology becomes more prevalent in classrooms and as the emphasis on engaged learning continues to escalate, the need for artifact collection or document analysis will be even more obvious. Historically, schools and districts have designed and used classroom observation to collect information and evidence regarding verbal and direct forms of teaching. To get the

richer picture of *all* that is involved in teaching, evaluators must use techniques that can reflect the kind of decisions that teachers are making when they plan and implement the full range of activities that define contemporary teaching. Hence, the majority of newly designed systems are requiring some form of artifact collection for beginning teachers during their first two years of employment.

What to Collect. Schools and districts must make some decisions about the form and nature of artifact collection. What should teachers collect? What will be included in the collection is determined by the supervisor and the teacher, based on the context of instruction. Many variables would be considered in these decisions: content, grade level, class size, district expectations for curriculum alignment, facilities, and availability of instructional aids, including access to technology. Figure 8.6 (p. 91) lists possible artifacts for the collection.

How Long to Collect. How long will the collection period last? The collection period would also be determined by the teacher and supervisor. Most would be for a minimum of one week to the time needed to complete a full unit of instruction. For an elementary teacher, most collections would be around a single content area such as reading/language arts. For a middle or high school teacher, the collection would focus on a single class or a week for a class of the teacher's least able students and a week of collection from the class with his most able students. This encourages a review of a teacher's decisions over different classes with a range of students and can provide some evidence as to the teacher's attentiveness to equity issues. How are the artifacts collected? It is the teacher's responsibility to collect those things that the supervisor and the teacher have

FIGURE 8.5
Years One and Two

East Grand Rapids School District
Required activities for beginning teachers include:

An Initial Staff Development Meeting

Before October 1, a building administrator will meet with all nontenured teachers as a group to review the Initial Staff Development expectations, professional portfolio collections, and evaluation time lines. At this time, the administrator will provide teachers with copies of all evaluation forms.

An Individual Development Plan

A building administrator will meet with each teacher to develop an Individual Development Plan based on the Standards for Effective Teaching (Teacher Development Form).

Formal Observations

Two formal observations will be conducted before March 15. Each of these observations will have a pre-observation conference. The teacher must complete and be ready to discuss the Pre-observation Form with the administrator at these conferences (Pre-observation Form). At least one of the formal observations will be conducted before the end of the first semester.

One of the formal observations will be of an extended duration. At the elementary level, this two- or three-hour observation will include classroom management and transition procedures. At the secondary level, the administrator will observe the same class period across consecutive days. (Classroom Observation Form)

The other formal observation will be a minimum of forty minutes at the elementary level or one class period at the secondary level. Additional formal observations may be scheduled at the discretion of the administrator (Classroom Observation Form).

A post-observation conference must be conducted within three working days of each of the observations. The purposes for the post-observation conferences are to:

1. Review the lesson(s) with a focus on student learning
2. Reinforce the strengths of the teaching performance
3. Identify areas for improvement
4. Offer specific feedback on classroom management
5. Review the professional development portfolio
6. Direct the new teacher toward relevant professional development opportunities
7. Provide opportunities for self-reflection

Evaluation forms will be completed by the administrator following the conference with the teacher (Evaluation Form and Summative Evaluation Form).

The administrator will make informal observations during the year which will be used as sources of information for the summative evaluation.

agreed to collect. Many teachers report that the simplest way to do this is to keep a box near their desk. The box gets a copy of everything the students get. The teacher then organizes the materials by sequencing them by day or topic and by the order of events (unit plan, daily plan, materials selected or developed to support instructional outcomes, samples of student work on the selected materials, etc.). This type of collection is an extended version of the providing of material used as part of a single lesson that is often requested as

---

FIGURE 8.6
A Sample of Artifacts for Possible Inclusion in a Beginning Teacher's Collection

- Class schedules
- Seating charts
- Semester and unit plans
- Daily plans
- Activity descriptions
- Classroom rules and discipline procedures
- Student achievement data
- Copies of quizzes and tests
- Copies of grade book
- Examples of student work
- Examples of written feedback
- Student profiles
- Copies of handouts and worksheets
- Reading lists
- Diagrams and photographs of room
- Parent and student surveys
- Logs of parent contacts
- Samples of messages to parents
- Video and audio records of student performances

---

a part of a preconference before an observation. Artifact collection is also often used as a part of any form of required portfolio development. If a district decides to require portfolios for beginning teachers, then the collection put together for this evaluation activity would become a part of the portfolio.

The Artifact Conference. Who will be involved in reviewing the artifacts? Depending on the size of the district or school and the availability of other staff to participate, supervisors will often invite a veteran teacher in the same grade level or content area, a department head, a lead teacher or team leader, a content supervisor from the central office, or the beginning teacher's mentor. Generally, the more perspectives within the discussion, the more productive and useful the process becomes.

Summative or Formative? Will the supervisor evaluate the artifacts, or will they be used as a formative experience? Figure 8.7 (pp. 92–93) provides a set of guidelines for reviewing instructional artifacts or documents. Most supervisors use this activity as a formative experience. The conference can be driven by the questions posed in the guidelines and by supervisors' questions designed to encourage the teacher to express the process they went through in determining the type and purpose of supporting or supplementary materials or aids that are reflected in the collection.

Most experienced supervisors report that the level of conversation and reflection in the artifact conference is quite high and that the beginning teachers' willingness to fully participate and benefit from the conference is notably increased if the process is conducted as a professional collaboration rather than as a summative evaluation event. The evaluator should take notes of the discussion and should provide a copy to the teacher. In addition, the evaluator could ask the teacher to provide a short reflective write-up of the conference as a way to bring some closure to the activity and to provide another opportunity to encourage the development of good professional habits.

Although the artifacts conference and the conversation it generates should be directed by a collegial, collaborative feeling, the whole process does provide evidence of the teacher's capacity and inclination to meet the district's teaching standards. The direct involvement of the supervisor in classroom observation and

FIGURE 8.7
Guidelines for Reviewing the Artifacts of Teaching—Conducting a Document Analysis

Artifacts are defined as simple objects, usually a tool or ornament, showing human workmanship or modification as distinguished from a natural object. The artifacts of teaching include any instructional materials or directions employed by teachers to facilitate student learning. Types may vary from commercially prepared textbooks and learning aids, such as maps, software packages, and science kits; to teacher-improvised demonstrations, tests, and worksheets; to the use of educational technology hardware and software.

In considering educational quality, artifacts must be learner oriented and designed to meet a specific outcome or standard. Artifacts are most helpful if they are designed with built-in flexibility permitting updating or adaptation to specific ability levels and uses.

CONTENT

Quality of artifacts can be considered from the point of view of content or essential meaning. Artifacts should be valid, relevant, and current. Some considerations related to quality of content are:

1. *Information:* Is the artifact materially accurate and authoritative?

2. *Areas of Controversy:* If relevant, are alternatives clearly acknowledged?

3. *Appropriateness:* Is the content appropriate for the intended audience? Is it appropriate in detail to the level of the learner and program or lesson objectives?

4. *Relevance and Validity:* Is the content relevant to the purpose of the lesson?

5. *Motivation:* Does the artifact content stimulate interest to learn more about the subject? Does it encourage ideas for using the material?

6. *Application:* Does the artifact serve as a model for applying learning outside the classroom?

7. *Clarity:* Is the content free of regional idioms, jargon, or specialized expressions that would limit its understandability?

8. *Conciseness:* Is the artifact free of superfluous material? Does it stick to the point?

DESIGN AND CONTEXT

Design of artifacts should include characteristics that are conducive to learning. Design should proceed from an analysis of the content of the lesson or local standards or benchmarks. Appropriate artifacts are those that are linked to local standards or benchmarks. The quality of an artifact is the product of its design characteristics, its relevance to identified outcomes, and its application to content.

Objectives for Artifact Design

1. *Meaningfulness:* Does the artifact clearly support the learning outcomes? If so, is this apparent to the learners?

2. *Appropriateness:* Are the artifacts appropriate to the needs of the skill levels of the intended learners? Are time constraints considered in the artifact's design?

Design Characteristics

1. *Sequencing:* Is the artifact itself sequenced logically? Is it employed at the appropriate point in the presentation?

2. *Instructional Strategies:* Is the artifact format appropriate to the students and the teaching approach? Does the artifact's construction incorporate sound learning principles?

3. *Engagement:* Does the artifact actively engage the learner? Does it reinforce the content with appropriate practice and feedback opportunities?

(continued)

FIGURE 8.7
(continued)

AESTHETIC CONSIDERATIONS

Aesthetic considerations include production and the qualities that enhance or detract from instructional effectiveness of the artifacts.

Quality of Communication

1. *Medium Selection:* Is the best medium used for meeting each specified outcome and presenting each item of content (e.g. motion pictures, videotape, textbook, teacher-prepared handout)?

2. *Economy of Time:* Is the learner's time wasted by such things as verbosity, unnecessary introduction and/or summary, or ad lib conversation without educational substance or purpose?

3. *Pace:* Is the pace appropriate to the intended audience, neither too fast nor too slow, throughout the presentation? Does the pace vary inversely with difficulty of content?

4. *Aids to Comprehension:* Are directions clearly explained? Are unfamiliar terms spelled out?

Technical Production

1. *Visual Quality:* Are subjects adequately illuminated? Do the visuals show all educationally significant details? Is composition uncluttered? Does it help the learner to recognize important content? Are essential details identified through the appropriate use of highlighting, color, tone, contrasts, position, motion, and other pointing devices? Is type size of the text legible at the anticipated maximum viewing distance?

2. *Narration:* Is the pace of the delivery appropriate for the intended audience? Can the audio component be clearly heard?

3. *Physical Quality:* Is the artifact durable, attractive, and simple? Are size and shape convenient for use?

---

their equal involvement in the review and discussion of the artifacts/documents used to support instruction and student learning are the primary reasons why these two sources of data assume such an important role as evidence in assessing performance in relationship to the teaching standards. These two methods also have reasonable levels of utility in that they are usable within the context of complicated and busy work environments.

Other Sources of Data

Schools and districts may consider other techniques for collecting important information.

Use of these other techniques depends on the amount of evidence the school or district wants to generate and the degrees of support and training it wants to provide new staff. These decisions will generally be made on the basis of staff time, availability of fiscal and personnel resources, and state or local contractual requirements. Additional options and activities range from journals to portfolios to mentoring programs.

Required Journals

Educators have long understood that journal writing improves reflective skills and encourages reflection to become a habit (Dietz, 1998).

Many districts have required beginning teachers to keep a journal as part of their evaluation program for year one and year two. When this is a required activity, districts ask that the supervisor and mentor meet with the teacher at least once during the year to have the teacher read selected entries from his journal. This is an opportunity to hear what the teacher is thinking and feeling and allows the supervisor, through the conversation generated by the teacher's comments, to behave in a more supportive and reinforcing way than is often possible in more evaluative environments. In most cases, this type of writing is built around entries that are reactions to everyday events in the life of the new teacher. Other types of journals have become popular; teachers use these in several school-related, growth-producing activities. In *Journals as Frameworks for Change*, Dietz (1998) offers a definition and a description of the following types of journals:

- *Action Research Journal:* Assesses the effect of informal research on student learning.
- *Professional Growth Journal:* Focuses on learning, collaboration, and assessment.
- *Staff Development Journal:* Monitors the implementation process used by coaches and mentors.
- *School Portfolio Journal:* Describes and reflects on various school programs and initiatives.
- *Study Group Journal:* Expands and deepens understanding of a theory or practice.

As suggested in Chapter 5, a teacher evaluation system committed to maximizing the professional growth of teachers should seriously consider including a focused approach to structured reflection on practice. Few practices are more effective at this than the use of journals.

Portfolios

Teaching portfolios are an increasingly popular activity for both evaluation and professional development.

Portfolio Characteristics. At its most basic, a teaching portfolio is a collection of information about a teacher's practice. Wolf, Lichtenstein, and Stevenson (1997) identify the key features of a teaching portfolio:

- A portfolio should be structured around sound professional teaching standards, and individual and school goals.
- A portfolio should contain carefully selected examples of both student and teacher work that illustrates key features of a teacher's practice.
- The contents of a portfolio should be framed by captions and written commentaries that explain and reflect on the contents of the portfolio.
- A portfolio should be a mentored or coached experience, in which the portfolio is used as a basis for ongoing professional conversations with colleagues and supervisors.

With these features as the framework for the purpose and the construction of a teaching portfolio, the use of this activity within a Track I system becomes attractive.

Formative or Summative? Most school districts that have required portfolios within the evaluation system view it as primarily a professional development activity used within an induction program. It can be used as a summative evaluation tool, but to do so requires a much more structured process and a complex set of assessment strategies. The assessment component requires clear criteria, an established set of valid and reliable scoring rubrics, and extensive training for the evaluators in order to assure fairness and reliability. These considerations can all be met, but they are often beyond the capacity or the will of a local district.

The use of portfolios as a professional development experience, especially for teachers new to a district, would seem to have extraordinary potential. Burke (1997) and Dietz (1998) both contend that portfolios have the capacity to present an authentic view of teaching and learning over time, thus offering a more complete and valid portrait of how teachers think and act. The creation of a teaching portfolio provides teachers, especially beginners, with a structure and a process for documenting and reflecting on their practice. This is the essence of professional learning.

Mentoring Programs

Many states already have in place required mentor programs for local districts, or they provide certain incentives to local districts to encourage them to establish mentoring activities. Even if they are not in states with required or encouraged mentoring, most districts that are developing new evaluation systems are including a required mentoring component within the new design.

Typically, mentors are expected to do the following with their assigned teacher:

• Help beginners learn to meet the procedural demands of the school.
• Provide moral and emotional support and function as sounding boards for new ideas.
• Provide access to other classrooms so that novices can observe other teachers and begin to know and understand the different models of teaching that can exist within a school.

• Share their own knowledge about new materials, planning strategies, curriculum development, and teaching methods.
• Assist teachers with classroom management and discipline.
• Help beginners understand the implications of student diversity for teaching and learning.
• Engage teachers in self-assessment and reflection on their own practice.
• Provide support and professional feedback as beginners experiment with new ideas and strategies.

Figure 8.8 describes a mentor program that is included within the evaluation document of a local school district. It is a good illustration of the issues involved in developing a mentoring program and of the way schools and districts can incorporate the program into the design of a Track I model.

Providing Summative Feedback

This chapter has focused on providing information and possible direction for district evaluation committees as they design the beginning teacher evaluation track within the full evaluation system. Schools and districts must make decisions about establishing a set of valid teaching standards and methods to be used for both evidence gathering and for supporting professional learning. In addition, they must determine the best ways for recording and giving feedback to the teacher.

Training, Training, Training

As suggested in this and previous chapters, any successful evaluation system must provide for training in understanding and

---

FIGURE 8.8
The Mentorship Program

Program Guidelines

1. Building administrators must have a commitment to the Mentorship Program.

2. Participation as a teacher mentor should be voluntary.

3. A mentor will be an experienced professional in the East Grand Rapids Public Schools.

4. A required half-day training session for mentors and mentees will be scheduled each year and take place prior to the first day of school. Mentors will receive the hourly compensation for this training session.

5. School-based teacher mentors should be given adequate time, resources, and support to perform their mentorship role, such as:

   • Release mentors and new teachers from non-instructional duties,

   • Schedule common preparation times once or twice a week for mentor(s) and new teacher(s) to discuss issues of concern to new teachers, and

   • Arrange for mentors and new teachers to share a common break time or lunch period for informal interaction.

6. Adequate time to visit other grade levels, classrooms, or schools should be given.

7. The critical and specialized role of teacher mentors should be acknowledged. Mentors have a maximum of $250 that is available to them for professional development opportunities. In addition, the mentor may select one of the following options as a stipend:

   • A $150 remuneration for the school year, or

• One compensatory day per semester (total of two [2] per school year), with such days to be approved by the building administrator of the mentor.

Important Characteristics of Mentor Teachers

It is expected that the mentor teacher will:

• Have demonstrated excellence in teaching and/or knowledge of a specific field of study,

• Have three to five years teaching experience, and have participated in professional development to remain current and maintain a high level of expertise,

• Be an active and open listener, sensitive and responsive to the ideas of others,

• Be an active participant in the role as mentor for the duration of the probationary period,

• Be competent in communication skills and have demonstrated successful "people skills,"

• If possible, be a practitioner in the same certification or specialty area as the new teacher with whom she is paired, and be located in the same building.

Areas of Training Considered Essential for Mentors

• To understand and apply the role, purpose, and process of mentoring including social, emotional, and instructional support

• To develop a written new teacher/mentor plan with administrative support and guidelines

• To develop skills effective in collaborative practice

• To acquire the knowledge of resources available for professional development

---

implementing the teaching standards, as well as training in implementing data-collection methods. During the training designed to improve observation skills, artifact and document analysis, portfolio use, and mentoring skills, there is often a component on learning conferencing skills and the appropriate ways to provide verbal feedback. In developing or selecting training programs for the supervisors and staff involved in new evaluation procedures, districts should be sure that these areas are covered.

Selecting Instruments

One area that is often neglected in evaluation programs is the instrumentation that will be used to provide the record of summative judgments. The final summative evaluation of a staff member carries considerable weight and importance. Supervisors normally present summative evaluations in a final conference; the supervisor also gives verbal descriptions and justifications for the judgments provided on · the evaluation document. This document can be some form of rating scale, a written narrative, or a combination of the two. For the person being evaluated, her willingness to accept and learn from the experience depends on several subtle factors: the way the evaluator develops a judgment of her performance; the form that shapes the way the evaluator presents the judgment; and the way the evaluator provides justification for the decision.

The use of rating scales within teacher evaluation systems has always been problematic. The most frequently mentioned difficulties revolve around their susceptibility to rater bias, the halo effect, and leniency, as well as serious questions about validity. This does not mean that local districts should not use them, but it is a suggestion that if scaling instruments are to be used, they should be carefully constructed so as to minimize the most common problem areas. The most useful and reliable form of rating can be accomplished by using behaviorally anchored rating scales (BARS). Figure 8.9 shows such a scale, which was developed for use in rating performance based on

the domains and components of Danielson's (1996) framework.

The complex process of developing and validating the written descriptions that anchor the various ratings requires more time and expertise than is often available in local districts. This is another argument for taking advantage of work already done by people or organizations who have the expertise and the resources.

Importance of a Narrative

Too be most effective, feedback on summative judgments should also include a narrative component. The narrative format allows for more extended and more fully described explanations of judgments that have been made and provides an opportunity for a more focused approach on those areas that are most relevant for each individual. A narrative provides a clearer and "lighter" approach to evaluation while still providing the opportunity for descriptive problem identification and remedial recommendations.

Borrowing from work originally done in dealing with written critiques in art (Meux, 1974), we recommend that all written summative feedback operate from a simple model of *valuing*. The model states that no value statement or value term should be used unless it is accompanied by example, anecdote, illustration, or description. These become the facts to support the value. This concept allows administrators to use the descriptive data collected during the required activities within the system as the facts to support the judgments which must accompany the required summative portion of the Track I system.

We think that the use of a validated BARS instrument that contains descriptive anchors

FIGURE 8.9
Sample of a Behaviorally Anchored Rating Scale (BARS)

Domain I: Planning and Preparation
Component 1a: Demonstrating Knowledge of Content and Pedagogy

Elements:
- Knowledge of content
- Knowledge of prerequisite relationships
- Knowledge of content-related pedagogy

Element	Level of Performance			
	Unsatisfactory	Basic	Proficient	Distinguished
Knowledge of content	Teacher makes content errors or does not correct content errors students make.	Teacher displays basic content knowledge but cannot articulate connections with other parts of the discipline or with other disciplines.	Teacher displays solid content knowledge and makes connections between the content and other parts of the discipline and other disciplines.	Teacher displays extensive content knowledge, with evidence of continuing pursuit of such knowledge.
Knowledge of prerequisite relationships	Teacher displays little understanding of prerequisite knowledge important for student learning of the content.	Teacher indicates some awareness of prerequisite learning, although such knowledge may be incomplete or inaccurate.	Teacher's plans and practices reflect understanding of prerequisite relationships among topics and concepts.	Teacher actively builds on knowledge of prerequisite relationships when describing instruction or seeking causes for student misunderstanding.
Knowledge of content-related pedagogy	Teacher displays little understanding of pedagogical issues involved in student learning of the content.	Teacher displays basic pedagogical knowledge but does not anticipate student misconceptions.	Pedagogical practices reflect current research on best pedagogical practice within the discipline but without anticipating student misconceptions.	Teacher displays continuing search for best practice and anticipates student misconceptions.

for each possible rating, accompanied by a required narrative that provides supporting commentary for the judgments presented, would offer the best chance to promote a successful closure to the Track I evaluation process.

9

Track II—The Professional Development Track

Professional development is the process by which competent teachers achieve higher professional competence and expand their understanding of self, role, context, and career (Duke & Stiggins, 1990). What influences a teacher to move toward increased professional growth? We find that it is not only the teacher's own motivation, awareness, and imagination, but also the policies and practices of the schools in which she teaches. Schon (1983, p. 338), in discussing the organizational conditions that promote reflective practice, noted the importance of "flexible procedures, differentiated responses, and decentralized responsibility for judgment and action." These conditions are at the heart of the design of Track II—professional growth.

Most teachers are neither probationary nor marginal. Consequently, the professional growth track becomes the dominant strand within the evaluation system. This track could be the norm for the majority of the staff (90 percent or more in many districts), with the following characteristics:

- The most experienced staff (average age for tenured teachers in many states and districts is in the mid-40s, with 15 or more years of experience).

- The most confident ("I have ways of doing things that work for me").
- The most vocal, opinionated, and influential (this group includes the union leadership and the group that exerts the majority of informal leadership).

In addition, new designs for this track diverge from traditional evaluation processes much more than do the Track I and Track III strands. Consequently, local evaluation committees must pay particular attention to the design of this program. Fortunately, several new systems have been in place long enough to offer guidelines for other districts to use. We presented some of the general guidelines in previous chapters. Lessons and experiences from these pioneering systems have helped shape our ideas and suggestions presented in this chapter.

Clarifying the Purpose of Track II

Track II programs imply an acceptance of alternative forms of assessment and a commitment to change the evaluation system. The real issue for a local evaluation committee is how to determine the relationship between formative and summative evaluation and the amount of time, energy, and resources given to each. We believe that schools can promote both quality assurance *and* professional learning in the same evaluation system—and that Track II is the place to do it. A typical purpose statement for Track II might look like this:

> The purpose of the professional growth track is to provide a structured, supportive, and collaborative environment to promote professional learning that will further the district's mission and enhance student learning. This track will provide a continuous cycle of assessment to ensure that all tenured staff continue to meet the district's standards for effective teaching.

Who Is Involved and When?

Obviously, this track is designed for all tenured teachers. The district must make decisions about whether the track will be optional, what kind of schedule it will follow, and how much involvement is expected from the supervisor. (Note: We use the term *supervisor* for conciseness; some schools and districts may use other forms of supervision and review, such as peer review teams, as described previously).

Will Track II Be Optional?

Districts must decide whether involvement in the professional development system will be voluntary or required. Some districts decide that not all teachers should have to be involved. Veterans may choose to only go through the summative activity on the established schedule (every two, three, or four years) and can opt out of the "other years" activities. This issue is usually raised by the union representatives on the evaluation committee and often reflects concerns regarding the amount of

time the formative activities will take, a lack of trust in the administration's capability to effectively handle the formative processes, or other issues regarding treatment of veteran teachers that find their way to the evaluation committee. Each context is different, and each district must decide on this issue based on the local conditions and past histories.

But good evidence is available to support the idea that professional growth is enhanced when others assist a teacher to heighten awareness of daily practice (Hawley & Valli, 1999). Without structured procedures that support and require outside input, teachers' capacity to grow is limited by their individual perspective. Schools and districts should consider professional development and professional learning a required part of teacher evaluation, not a separate activity like staff development or inservice training. Professional development research, including studies that solicit feedback from teachers involved in new systems, overwhelmingly support all staff being required to go through the system together (see Hawley & Valli).

Is Involvement Continuous or Cycled?

The two sample systems outlined in the appendixes include continuous involvement in Track II. Once a district fully implements the new system, there is no down time for teachers. There may be some cycle of formal summative assessment built into the system (every third or fourth year, for example), but involvement in the formative and summative components is continuous.

The two systems have a different approach to handling summative assessment. The Addison district views summative evaluation as a continuous process created by the daily interactions of teachers and administrators. There is no formal summative assessment activity in this system outside of Track I and Track III. When teachers in Track II reach some form of closure with their professional development plan, they and their supervisor build a new plan and establish a new time line.

In the Newport News system, tenured teachers in Track II undergo a summative assessment once every four years. This summative assessment includes traditional observation, focusing on the teaching standards, and a review of a teacher's portfolio that serves as the documentation of the three-year formative process in which the teacher has been involved. At the end of the summative year, the process starts again. Whatever design that a local district uses, it should ensure that tenured teachers are continuously involved in Track II.

What Is the Level of Involvement of the Supervisor in the Process?

For summative evaluation, there's an easy answer to this question: The principal or her designee has the right and the responsibility to summatively assess teachers in their building. So unless the district practices some form of peer review or peer evaluation for summative evaluation, the supervisor is always involved.

The supervisor's role in the professional development activities in Track II is often less clear. The language of professional development and professional learning often proposes that teachers determine, implement, and complete their own professional development plans. Districts must decide where the supervisor fits into this process. In most cases, districts build in a significant role for their administrators in the formative processes. The required processes include the involvement of the supervisor in the

final determination of the focus and the components of the teacher's plan.

In both the Addison system and the Newport News system (see the appendixes), the teacher or a team of teachers takes the initiative to identify the focus of their efforts in the formative program. This identification can come from self-assessments, from building or district goals, from student learning concerns, or from personal motivation to gain new skills or to acquire new knowledge. Then the teacher (or teachers) meet with the supervisor in a conference to review and refine the plan.

At the conference, the teacher or group of teachers can assure the supervisor that plans fall within the parameters of the district's professional development plans. For example, here are some requirements for many such plans:

• They attend to building or district initiatives.
• They address student learning.
• They focus on teaching and learning.
• They include plans for identifying outcomes.
• They involve collaborative work.
• They are reasonable in terms of resource and time available.

The role of the supervisor is to ask good questions, encourage tightening or broadening the scope of the plan as may be needed, share ideas about ways to facilitate the implementation of the plan, or identify resources that may be available to support the plan. The idea is to support and enhance the plan, not reject it.

Most teachers will take this task seriously and will develop high-quality plans. What they need most is an experienced and trained professional supervisor who can help focus and support their plan. Supervisors should not be asked to play the role of summative evaluators and then have no role in the required formative experiences. This will only widen the gap between supervisors and their staffs. A professional learning community must involve everyone in the school.

The Design of the System

Once the purpose of Track II has been determined and the decisions about the levels of involvement are made, the procedures and processes that will shape the system can be determined.

Summative Component

Decisions on the nature and extent of the summative component in Track II may be driven by state mandates requiring a specific form of structured evaluation event. Districts will need to decide if the state mandate will support its vision of what Track II should accomplish. If state requirements would inhibit this vision, districts should consider asking to have it waived. This is becoming a more prevalent action as states have become increasingly willing to support waiver requests. If the state has a flexible policy on local evaluation procedures, then the district can proceed with determining the format for the summative experiences that most comfortably fit its desired purpose for Track II. There are several options from which to choose.

Cycled Summative Assessments. The Newport News system (see Appendix B) offers an excellent example of a cycled summative experience. Every fourth year, a tenured teacher receives a summative evaluation. In Newport News, the process for summative evaluation is the same process the nontenured, probationary

teachers go through in Track I. It includes the following:

- A conference at the beginning of the evaluation year to review the standards and the procedures.
- A teacher self-assessment to identify areas on which the teacher may want to focus special attention.
- Two formal observations.
- The submission of a portfolio that contains documentation of the teacher's performance.
- A final conference held to discuss the evaluation and to meet the district requirements for filed documentation (i.e., proper forms completed, the administrator's signature, the teacher's signature, and the placing of the completed evaluation in the teacher's district file).

The judgment by the administrator that performance meets the district's standards for teaching becomes the trigger that continues the teacher's involvement in the formative process over the next three years. An administrator's judgment that the standards were not being met to a satisfactory degree could lead to a teacher's being placed in the Track III assistance program. This set of activities is representative of what most districts who require cycled summative evaluations are doing.

The decisions about how supervisors make summative judgments and document them are similar to those for probationary teachers (see Chapter 8). For example, supervisors should follow the Track I observation process: a preconference, the formal observation, and the post-conference. In this process, again, certain forms are useful: the preconference planning form, the observation guide for use during the classroom visit, and the reflective form for the post-conference. This is the best way to ensure that the observations are as reliable, valid, and useful as possible. The number of observations would be determined by time, resources, and personnel constraints. In most districts, the number of observations for tenured staff would be no more than one or two in the summative year.

The summative feedback mechanisms could also be the same for Track II as they were for Track I. The same behaviorally anchored scale that is provided in Danielson's (1996) book *Enhancing Professional Practice: A Framework for Teaching*, or a locally developed adaptation could serve as a source of feedback on the teacher's performance in meeting the standards. If a district decides that a portfolio would be helpful in the summative process, then the portfolio could be a compilation of work and assessments developed over the three-year formative process or it could cover only evidence of effort and outcomes developed specifically for the summative year. In either case, the portfolio, along with the judgments made as a result of observations, would be the data source used to generate the ratings. As recommended in Chapter 8, a written narrative should accompany the ratings. Some districts decide that a narrative alone is sufficient feedback on a tenured teacher's performance. This would also be a local decision based on the perceptions held by the committee as to the relative merits of scales, narratives, or a combination.

Continuous Informal Appraisals. The Addison district's decision on how it would handle the summative component within Track II offers another option that several districts are using. A statement is provided in the description of Track II that indicates that all teachers are continuously held up against the standards (see Appendix A). In Addison's view, summative evaluation is not an activity that occurs according to a cycle, but is an ongoing process. For them, the daily interactions among administrators, teachers, students, parents, support staff, and the community are a rich source of feedback that help form the professional judgments that characterize summative evaluations. This form of holistic professional judgment may include informal drop-ins or walk-throughs of classroom, but does not involve mandated classroom observations of tenured teachers.

In districts that choose this format for their evaluation system, all tenured teachers are automatically in Track II. They remain fully involved in Track II unless the supervisor begins to have concerns about the teacher's performance. At this point, the supervisor contacts the teacher, raises the concern, and determines with the teacher how they should address the concerns. This could involve scheduling classroom observations, but only if observation would fit the type of concern being raised. This transition between Track II and Track III is often labeled the awareness phase. (See Chapter 10 for a description of the Track III assistance program.) If the teacher positively addresses or clarifies the concern, involvement in Track II continues normally. If the problem is real and cannot be resolved during the initial contacts between the teacher and the supervisor, then exactly the same action occurs as it would in a cycled summative model: The supervisor or peer review team moves the teacher into the assistance program.

This option frees administrators from conducting formal observations on tenured teachers. In districts that do this, administrators feel that they have more time for working with beginning teachers, for assisting tenured staff experiencing difficulties, and for keeping some involvement with the professional development activities of the tenured staff. The down side of this option is that it moves away from commonly held views about the value of and the need for direct and structured administrative involvement in summative evaluation. It is also contrary to belief in the important role that regular summative feedback can play in helping teachers become more thoughtful and self-evaluative about their work. Within the parameters of its local context, a district committee needs to decide which option or an adaptation of one of the options best fits its identified purpose and its capacity.

Formative Process

Districts have several options available for use in designing formative evaluation activities. As usual, these decisions will be shaped by the time, resources, and levels of commitment that are available within the district. The district must answer several questions as committees decide what the local evaluation system will include.

Is Assessment a Part of the Formative Process? Formative assessment is, after all, an *assessment*. What often pass for formative assessments are cursory examinations of work completed without the benefit of informed judgments, feedback, or structured reflection. Judgments made and shared in the formative process are not high-stakes activities, as they might be in summative assessment. But formative judgments play a necessary role in the

learning and growing process that defines formative work. Effective frameworks for the design of professional development all involve some noticeable outcome. The most successful systems include mechanisms to ensure that schools use some type of formative assessment as a part of the required analysis and reflection on the outcomes.

Should Outcomes Be Product Based with an Extended Impact? Most schools and districts that use the formative segment of Track II encourage or require some final outcome, or product. These products represent closure on a set of timed actions or activities that are implemented to meet or demonstrate progress toward a predetermined goal or plan. Products can be as obvious as a completed portfolio, a live or taped demonstration of newly acquired skills, the written results of an action research project, the conducting of a series of workshops for other faculty, or the completion of a set of integrated lessons or units. Outcomes can also be less obvious "products," such as completing a college course, attending two workshops, or visiting other schools to observe what they are doing. One caution: When schools or districts allow these less obvious products, it can be more difficult to determine the usefulness, effect, or value of what occurred. Districts need to decide if the system is going to insist that goals or plans should result in an obvious product that allows for informed and useful assessment (formative, not summative), for productive feedback and for self-reflection.

Some districts write into their descriptions of the required procedures that the products or outcomes sought would have an extended impact. This means that the product would have value beyond that gained by the individual or the team who produced it. Examples might include workshops given to other staff, based on what the individual or team learned; lessons or units designed that can be used by others; or action research results that can be used to review or change school policies or practices. This idea may not need to be written in as a necessary ingredient in developing a goal or a plan, but a district may want to introduce school staffs to the idea of broad-impact products of formative evaluation.

Should There Be Parameters on the Development of Goals or Plans? The local evaluation committee must discuss the range of acceptable plans. We previously suggested that the supervisor review individual or team-developed plans or goals to ensure that the plans fall within the established parameters. Most districts set some guidelines for acceptable plans—such as the following:

- "All plans and goals must be linked to the Standards for Teaching."
- "Plans must support district, school, or department initiatives."
- "All goals and plans must include the potential effect of the work on student learning."

Other parameters could include requirements on such things as time lines for completion of the work (usually one-, two-, or three-year options); requirements that only certain activities be used (peer coaching, action research, or portfolio development); requirements that plans include the identification of a support team or study group; and requirements that plans result in the production of a professional development portfolio. In most cases, schools and districts would clarify these parameters on the directions listed within the Track II section

of the evaluation document or within the required forms. Figure 9.1 shows how the Bartholomew School Corporation (Columbus, Indiana) presented its parameters within a series of questions designed to guide teachers in building a professional growth plan.

What Activities Will the District Require or Permit Within the Professional Growth Track? New conceptions of effective professional development offer several activities that research has shown supports growth and reflective behavior in teachers (Hawley & Valli, 1999). District must decide if there will be limits on the options from which staff may choose as individuals or teams design their professional development plan. These guidelines shown in Figure 9.1 (p. 106) offer many options from which to choose (see "methods and strategies"). Figure 9.2 (p. 107) shows the form to be used in developing the plan description at the initial conference. It typifies the straightforward reporting document that is developed by local districts for describing the original plan.

Other districts have decided to limit the strategies/methods that teachers can use in developing the plan. Placing limits focuses the staff's activity to selected methods that the district and the committee feels can be most beneficial in promoting the desired professional learning outcomes of inquiry, growth, and reflection. Figure 9.3 (p. 108) shows the documentation options within the professional growth track as developed by the Cumberland-North Yarmouth, Maine, School District. They specifically limited the options to an action research project, a peer coaching experience, or the development of a professional growth portfolio. It was their feeling that by limiting the options, the time and resources would be available to provide ongoing training in these

FIGURE 9.1
Bartholomew Consolidated School Corporation
Professional Growth Plan: Guidelines for Development

A professional growth plan may be developed for an individual staff member; or a team of staff members may elect to collaboratively develop a plan. The plan may be for 1, 2, or 3 years. If a plan is for 2 or 3 years, an Annual Summary Appraisal will be completed. At the conclusion of the plan, a Final Summary Appraisal will be completed. Revisions to the plan may be completed annually.

Professional Growth Plan Element	Suggestion
• What **format** will be used? Format could include:	Working with an administrator, with peers, independently; multidisciplinary, grade level teams, department teams, or a combination of approaches
• What is the **goal** of your Professional Growth Plan? Goals could include:	Individual, team, building, or district goals that result in the continuous improvement of student learning
• What is the **time line** for your plan? Time line could include:	1-year, 2-year, or 3-year plan; include anticipated starting date of plan
• What **methods/strategies** will be used? Methods/strategies could include:	Action research, coaching, video taping, self-assessment, clinical supervision, mentoring, college courses, simulations, workshops, visitation days, conferences, classroom observations, teacher academies
• What are the **indicators of progress?** Indicators of progress could include:	Student work portfolios, videotapes of classes, peer observation, principal observation, parent responses, student responses, statistical measures, performance assessment, reflective journal entries, case study analysis, professional portfolios, benchmarks
• What **resources/support** are needed? Resources/support could include:	Classroom materials, student materials, journals, workshops, resources, books, collegial time, appropriate technology, mentoring, collegial support, release time, administrative support

three activities. The idea is that specific and intensive training in a set of acknowledged professional development practices would enhance the quality, the power, and the consistency of the plans and the desired outcomes.

This is an interesting notion that local evaluation committees should discuss and consider.

The following are the most commonly used professional development activities within Track II:

FIGURE 9.2
Bartholomew Consolidated School Corporation
Professional Growth Plan: Description

Staff member _____ Participant(s) _____

Building _____ Subject _____ Length of plan: 1 2 3 years

Format _____

Goal:

Describe how this will improve student learning

Year 1
1. Methods/Strategies

2. Indicators of Progress

3. Resources/Support Needed

Staff member(s) signature _____ Adminisrator signature _____

Starting date of plan _____ Today's date _____

Additional pages may be added . A word processor may be used to write the plan in lieu of this form.

- *Action Research*. Action research is done by individuals or groups of teachers who identify a problem and develop a workable solution. After the group identifies and defines the problem it intends to address, it develops an action plan and time line for the project. Members develop a strategy for gathering information about the problem. Once this information has been considered, the group makes changes and gathers and analyzes new data to determine the effects of the intervention. Teachers are then often called on to report their findings and share their insight with the rest of the faculty.

FIGURE 9.3
Maine School District #51—Documentation Options

Maine School Administrative District #51
Cumberland-North Yarmouth

To promote continuous professional growth in the interest of improving student learning, eligible teachers may select from the following options. Annual training in each of the three models will be provided by the district. The training will enable teachers to select the option that will help them achieve their goals. Teacher and evaluator work together to select the option that most closely relates to the teacher's goal.

Action Research

Classroom-Based Research

This option allows a teacher to work on a question he or she might have in regard to classroom performance, student needs, or the impact of various teaching methods on learning. The information gathered by the teacher is then used to improve teaching and student learning. Classroom based research can be self-directed or be done by a group of teachers who have a common interest/question to be researched.

Possible Areas for Research

- Questions on instruction
- Questions about students' perceptions about a task
- Questions about student performance
- Questions about teacher values
- Questions about the context in which a task is done

Advantages

- Based on individual needs/concerns
- More than one person can be involved
- Can be used to analyze effectiveness of programs

- Can be spread over the three years of professional development cycle

Peer Coaching

Peer coaching is the process through which two or more professional colleagues work together to share their knowledge of best instructional practices and to provide each other with feedback, support and assistance for the purpose of refining present teaching techniques and learning new skills.

A peer coach should be a trusted professional who communicates well, is open-minded, strives to improve his or her own teaching skills, is responsible, conscientious, and creative in the classroom.

The peer coaching process has three components within an observation cycle. The cycle will occur a minimum of two times during the implementation period.

Pre-conference

Teacher(s) and coach(es) meet to informally develop a common language and communication rapport. A decision is made when to do an observation, how the coach will be received in the classroom, and the role the coach will play while observing. An initial observation to the classroom should be made prior to the first observation to establish the relationship between participants in this process.

Observation

An observation is more than just watching a teacher work. An observation should be an objective reflection about a topic determined at the pre-conference. The observation should be purposeful, factual, value-free, specific, and nonjudgmental. The observer may use several methods of data

(continued)

**FIGURE 9.3
(continued)**

---

collection during the observation. These methods will be presented at teacher training sessions to be held yearly.

Post-Conference

At a post-conference, the coach is to provide the feedback in a helpful, nonthreatening manner. The teacher is to actively listen and to assess the data presented by the coach.

After the information has been given to the teacher, the coach may ask questions, be asked for suggestions or additional comments. Recognition and praise should be given for accomplishments and possible modifications could be suggested. The purpose of the post-conference is to help the

teacher refocus on the observation to prepare for the next coaching cycle.

Portfolio Development

A portfolio is a purposeful collection of a teacher's best work. Portfolios will include scholarly writings, articles of research, staff development from instructional workshops and seminars. The collection of data will reflect the goals of the district and be a selective one that highlights the distinctive features of that individual's approach to teaching. The portfolio will be a collaborative venture, reflecting the contributions of mentor, colleagues, and students. The portfolio will demonstrate a teacher's accomplishments over time and across a variety of experiences.

• *Curriculum Development.* This is the process of designing a curriculum or a component of the curriculum and analyzing the impact on student learning. Specific activities might include *deepening* the curriculum (rather than wide coverage, more in-depth work in fewer areas), refocusing curriculum to support *engaging* students in the work of the classroom, *integrating* the curriculum through cross-discipline conversations, and developing new ways of better *assessing* students on curriculum-based work.

• *Instructional Strategies Implementation.* This involves teacher(s) investigating particular instructional strategies, such as cooperative learning, problem-based learning, inclusion activities, and alternative classroom management techniques. This would be followed by the implementation of the strategy within the instructional program, and the documentation

and analysis of the effectiveness of the strategy on student learning.

• *Peer Consultation/Coaching.* This activity involves the training of teams of teachers to use clinical supervision to help each other grow professionally. It involves certain key characteristics:

– The process is observation-based: Colleagues observe each other teach.

– The observations are data-based: The observer records full information about the class observed.

– There is collaborative assessment: Each participant tries to identify patterns of teacher and learner behavior.

– There is a concern for student outcomes.

– The collaborative assessment is based on the goals and the desired outcomes established in the professional growth plan.

– The process involves a cycle of observation, conferences, and documentation.

• *Professional Growth Portfolios.* A portfolio can be a means of collecting, displaying, and reflecting on a professional growth experience, or it can be a professional development event of its own. Burke (1997) indicates that constructing professional development portfolios enables educators to do the following:

– Articulate their visions of teaching and learning.

– Develop professional goals and plans.

– Select learner-centered goals.

– Document progress in achieving the goals.

– Interact with peers throughout the process.

– Reflect on the learning experience and attainment of goals.

– Share insights with others.

According to Dietz (1998), portfolios provide added value: "A professional development portfolio provides teachers with a framework for initiating, planning, and facilitating their personal/professional growth while building connections between their interests and goals and those of the school."

• *Structured Professional Dialogue-Study Groups-Support Teams.* Small groups of teachers gather together regularly to hold focused discussions of a current development in education, to examine a school-based teaching or learning issue, to develop an individual or a team-based professional development plan, or to support and assist an individual teacher's required remediation action plan.

Can Goals or Plans Be Remedial? The major purpose of the formative process is the promotion of professional development (taking competent staff beyond competence) or professional learning (active involvement in learning within a collaborative and reflective community). The purpose is not to provide directed, structured remediation. In Track II, teachers take the initiative in identifying the desired focus for their efforts and sharing this with their supervisor for review.

It is certainly possible that some teachers, as a result of their self-assessment, decide they would like to focus their goals or plans on improving in an area in which they feel deficient. If the teacher is the instigator of this idea and if the plan of action, the nature of the product, and the means by which the outcomes or progress will be measured, all fit within the established parameters, then this could be viewed as a legitimate plan. On the other hand, it is unacceptable for the supervisor to change or reject a submitted plan to insert a remedial focus. If the supervisor feels strongly that a teacher has not met a required standard, then it should be handled within Track III.

Another violation of the spirit of Track II would occur when teachers develop *formative* goals or plans at the conclusion of a cycled *summative* event and when the supervisor focuses on problems or concerns identified as a result of the summative evaluation. If a summative evaluation identifies real or potential problems in meeting the district standards, then any action taken should be determined by the requirements of the assistance program. Local evaluation committees need to be sure that administrators and teachers understand the distinction between *remedial* plans and *professional development* plans. Districts should establish a process that allows for feedback from staff during the first several years of implementation of the new system, to ensure that schools or administrators are not misusing the formative Track II program.

Must Goals or Plans Be New Efforts? Most teachers are concerned about the amount of work that is involved in moving to a new evaluation system. This is especially true when a district is moving from a traditional evaluation program where everything is done *to* the teacher, and there is little work involved other than being observed and showing up for a conference every two to four years. Suddenly, the new system asks for heavy teacher involvement—giving the impression that now teachers, not administrators, are doing most of the work of evaluation. Districts must address this issue.

Most districts have found that they must allow and even encourage teachers to develop their Track II goals or plans around work or efforts in which they may already be involved. Examples of such efforts are (1) developing instructional activities that are going to be required in implementing a middle school model, (2) preparing for a new block scheduling plan, and (3) developing technology skills or applications that schools are already encouraging or requiring as part of a technology grant. If districts allow staff to form a group to write a team plan that will satisfy Track II requirements, teachers may form many teams around groups already in existence (e.g., grade-level teams, members of the school or district reading committee, colleagues from across high school departments who are already in conversation about the development of a humanities course).

Forming such interrelated teams will certainly not lower the power of the professional development goals or plans. In many respects, it helps to bring together a series of district or individually initiated projects that people often see as separate. It also offers teachers a way to fully participate in the professional development component of Track II without feeling that they must create new projects over and above all their other efforts.

How Might Districts Determine Time Frames for Plans? In systems that establish a cycled summative experience, the frequency of the summative year will determine the time allocated for the formative system (e.g., four-year cycle = one summative year + three years in the formative process). Districts that are using a more informal and continuous monitoring of performance will often offer staff the choice of establishing one-, two-, or three-year plans. In these cases, one of the parameters established for use by supervisors in reviewing the proposed plans is that the length of the requested time frame must fit the complexity and the potential of the plan. It would make sense for districts, even those that have a set period for the formative experiences, to allow teachers to set different time frames (see box, "Suggestions" for different types of goals or plans and what might be appropriate time lines).

Should Districts Allow Teams of Teachers to Develop Goals/Plans? Desired outcomes of many school improvement initiatives include bringing classroom practice out of isolation and increasing collaboration among staff. Many schools believe that they can accomplish these desired practices by allowing and encouraging teachers to form teams and develop one professional development plan or one set of goals for the group. Usually schools would define teams as groups of two to seven staff who come together around an idea of mutual interest or concern. The team develops the plan and

Suggestions for Supervisors and Teachers in Goal/Plan Setting

Setting Teaching/Learning Goals Derived from the Teaching Standards

Refining Current Practices (Improvement Goals). This type of goal fits a range of teaching areas, especially those that would be included under Domains 1, 2, and 3 in Danielson's (1996) framework. It could include work on improving a more basic skill (managing student behavior) or a more complex skill (engaging students in learning). The important thing here is that the teacher is indicating a desire to improve something she already does in her teaching. This type of goal would almost always be set by an individual rather than a team. The plan for this type of goal could involve classroom observation as a form of formative assessment or some form of artifact collection to demonstrate the desired improvement. This type of goal would generally be set for only one year.

Acquisition of New Skills or Knowledge (Renewal Goals). In acquiring new skills or knowledge to enhance the application of the teaching standards, it should be assumed that this type of goal will require some resources to support the gaining of the skill or the needed information. The plan would likely include some form of demonstration of the newly acquired skill or practice (presentation to other faculty, review by a support group or study group, written material distributed to others, or an actual or taped demonstration).

This type of goal could be set by an individual or a team. To maximize the use of building or district resources, the new skill or knowledge should be required to be directly related to the teaching standards or to building or district teaching and learning initiatives. In most situations, this would be a two- or three-year plan, to give time to acquire the new knowledge and to test its implementation.

Doing Things Differently (Redesign or Restructuring Goals). These goals will often be set as derivatives of the components of professional practice as stated in the standards. In settings different from traditional practice, the application of the standards might have more significance. Developing goals and plans that would lead to new ways of doing things (project-based learning, nongraded rooms, developing interdisciplinary teams in high schools) provides a new way of thinking about and demonstrating the importance of the teaching standards. This type of activity will almost certainly require additional resources and time. This work should be done by a team and never for less than two or three years. The product of this type of activity should include a rationale for the change, the desired student outcomes, a discussion of the possible implications of the new way of doing things for other parts of the system, and a plan for evaluating all relevant outcomes of the change.

(continued)

Setting Program or Curriculum Goals and Plans (from Content Standards or Within the Process of Developing Content Standards)

"Deepening" Goals (Organizing Curriculum Around Deepening Student Understanding). This type of goal would focus on moving from broad curriculum coverage to a deeper concept of curriculum that requires identifying what is most important for students to learn (i.e., focusing on themes or questions rather than sequences of facts). Teachers could work toward this goal individually or as a team. The product for this goal should include a rationale, what students should know and be able to do as a result of this work, and a plan for assessing student learning and evaluating the merit of the changes. This could be a one-, two-, or three-year goal, depending on the scope of the project.

"Integrating" Goals (Designing Learning Experiences to Assist Students in Connecting Ideas and Concepts Across Different Content Areas). These goals would focus on developing integrated lessons, units, and courses. This work could be done individually or in teams. Products should include rationale, desired student outcomes, necessary materials, recommended teaching practices, and a plan for assessing student learning and evaluating the merit of the activity. These goals should be for two or three years, depending on the scope of the effort.

"Engaging" Goals (Designing Learning Experiences to Engage Students). These goals would focus on developing curriculum plans, materials, and related activities that attend specifically to increasing the engagement of students in the work of the classroom. These would also include attempts to engage different groups of students, based on special needs, styles, or developmental stages. The product should include desired student outcomes, any curriculum materials needed, identification of the necessary teaching strategies and skills, and a plan for assessing student outcomes and the merit of the process. This could be done by an individual or a team over one, two, or three years, depending on the scope of the plan.

"Assessing" Goals (Designing Activities and Experiences Determining What Students Have Learned and What They Can Do). This type of goal would focus on developing new or alternative assessments to measure or describe student learning. This could be done individually or in teams. The product should include a rationale for developing the new assessment procedures, the student outcomes to be assessed, the measures and rubrics to be used, and the implications for curriculum and instruction. Depending on the complexity and scope of the assessment activity being developed, this could be a one-, two-, or three-year plan.

presents it to the supervisor just as an individual would. (Note: If teams are from the same school, their own administrator works with them; if the team members are from different schools, an administrator from one of the represented schools is designated as the administrator who will work with the group).

Another benefit of allowing teams is that it does reduce the number of conferences and follow-up activities that the administrator will be involved in during the formative years. Districts that allow teams to be involved in Track II activities report that the internal collaborations and the levels of professional reflection and conversation generated by the group are an added bonus to an already powerful professional learning experience. If a district prefers that individual teachers set their own goals or plans, then schools can build other team activities into the evaluation system—such as study groups or support teams. These activities produce the benefits of teaming while still maintaining individual requirements.

Documentation and Feedback in Track II

Earlier in this chapter, we suggested ways to deal with the documentation and feedback of the *summative* process that a district chooses to use in Track II. Handling the final experience in the professional development (*formative*) phase requires a different approach. The outcomes of the professional development process are not designed to demonstrate a person's teaching skill. The product or products should be the natural and logical outcome of a goal or a plan that is designed to promote learning for students and professional learning for the

teacher. The sources of evidence that are a part of the teacher's or the team's plan are there to provide feedback on the results of the effort and to promote the habits of inquiry and reflection.

Districts will normally expect some form of closure and documentation at the end of the established time frame. This most often would take the form of a final conference and some required narrative write-up that would be placed in a teacher's file. In some cases, the write-up would be placed in a professional development file that is kept at the school, rather than in the official file at the district level. Only summative forms would be placed in the official district file. This should be a local decision, based on how strongly the evaluation committee would feel about separating the professional development and summative processes.

Formative judgments should form the basis of the discussion and documentation of the outcomes of the teacher's established plan. Supervisors or peer review teams would make these judgments as *feedback* for discussion and reflection, not for summative purposes. The judgments would be based on determinations of the level of effort, the importance of the work, the level of involvement (if it is a team project), and the evidence of progress. The highlight of this concluding experience should be the conference, not the write-up. Final documentation, especially by the supervisor, should be done at the conclusion of the conference, not ahead of time.

The discussion, as driven by the work presented by the teacher or the team, allows opportunities for fuller explanation of outcomes and activities, for exchanges of ideas and possibilities, and for collaborative

---

FIGURE 9.4
Bartholomew Consolidated School Corporation
Professional Growth Plan Review

Staff member(s) _____

School _____ Date _____ Year 1 2 3

A. List the target goal(s) of the Professional Growth Plan.

B. List a descriptive summary of the process used in the Professional Growth Plan.

C. List vital results/outcomes from the Professional Growth Plan.

Staff member(s) comments:

Administrator comments:

Signatures:
Staff member(s) _____

Administrator _____ Date _____

Additional pages may be added if necessary. A word processor may be used in lieu of this form.

Copies: Staff member(s)   Principal   Personnel Director

---

judgments to be made and polished. The supervisor or peer review team can then complete the write-up, following an outline provided by all of the rich discussion at the conference. In effect, the conference becomes another source of evidence. Consequently, districts should design specific forms and documents to be completed as the culminating activity of the formative process. These forms will allow teachers and supervisors to participate in this kind of final experience.

Figure 9.4 illustrates the final review form for the Bartholomew School Corporation's Professional Growth Track. It is completed by the teacher (if done individually) or by the team, and the supervisor after the conference held at

---

FIGURE 9.5
Clarence Central Schools—Track II: Professional Development Plan (PDP) Formative Appraisal

This form is to be completed by individual team members in the final year of a team's Professional Development Plan (PDP).

Title of Professional Development Plan (PDP): _____

Staff Member: _____

Other Staff Member(s) on the Project: _____

_____

School: _____

Building Principal/Supervisor: _____

Date: _____

A. The following is a descriptive summary of the Professional Development Plan (PDP) that was submitted and completed by the above staff member(s).

B. The following is a statement of the individual staff member's thoughts about how this Professional Development Plan (PDP) has increased his/her effectiveness as a teacher and his/her students' success.

C. The following is a statement of the Building Principal's/Supervisor's thoughts, reactions, etc. regarding the Professional Development Plan (PDP) that was submitted and completed by the above staff member(s).

Clarence Central School District, New York

---

the end of the designated time frame. The form allows for a summary of what occurred and provides for the teacher's and supervisor's feedback on the completed experience. In the case of a team plan, the administrator makes copies of the final report and places them in each individual teacher's personnel file.

Figure 9.5 shows another example of a final write-up document. This form, developed by the Clarence Central, New York, School District, requires each individual team member to complete a reflective statement on what the team accomplished and what the individual teacher gained through this experience. A copy of each individual's comments goes into the teacher's personnel file.

The task of building a new teacher evaluation system in a local school district is a serious undertaking that demands a significant commitment of time and resources. We have found no better way to enhance and energize the work and the attitudes of the adults who work in the school. Using Track II activities as the locus of the primary professional development experiences of the staff will produce the type of professional learning that will benefit both teachers and students.

10

Track III—The Teacher Assistance Track

The purpose of Track III is to provide organizational support and assistance to teachers who are not meeting the district's teaching standards. The existence of this track is what makes it possible for Track II to focus on professional development rather than remediation.

In designing Track III, the evaluation committee should continue their focus on the spirit of quality assurance, with support, that characterized the beginning teacher program and the summative process within Track II. Educators should perceive of the assistance program in Track III as an in-house, good-faith effort on the part of the district. This track demonstrates the district's commitment to quality teaching by providing a supported, structured, and focused system of assistance to ensure that every staff member is meeting the district standards.

Who Should Be Involved in Track III?

This track should be developed to serve a group of tenured teachers who are often identified as *marginal teachers* (those who, in the professional judgment of an administrator, are experiencing difficulty in meeting one or more of the district's standards for effective teaching). This track is designed for the district's

tenured staff, not for the probationary staff. If probationary teachers are having problems in meeting the standards, administrators or peer review teams should deal with the problems through the established procedures in Track I.

Our experience suggests that in most districts, 2 to 5 percent of the total number of tenured staff should be involved with the assistance program. Obviously, this is a guideline, not a rule. Numbers of Track III teachers will vary, based on the rigor with which the district applies standards; the training the district provides to the staff; and the willingness of the district, the administrative staff, and—to some extent the teacher's union—to regard the assistance program as a necessary and important professional responsibility.

Two groups of teachers dominate those involved in the assistance track. The first group consists of teachers who are experiencing some trauma or stressful episode in their life. Divorce, serious illness, the death of a loved one, bankruptcy, family disputes, and some forms of depression and dependency—all these events can affect a teacher's performance in the classroom. When their problems result in failure to meet the teaching standards, then they enter the assistance program. This group of teachers tends to respond favorably to the attention, structure, and support of Track III initiatives.

The second group of teachers most frequently moved into the assistance program tends to be a small number of veteran staff who have been able to coast along in their performance because the district has never had a structured program for remediation. Traditional evaluation systems typically dealt with marginal teachers by using the district's summative evaluation forms (usually scales or narratives) every two to four years to remind them of their strengths and weaknesses or their areas of needed improvement. These systems usually had no systematic follow-up, provided no structured support systems, and applied no real pressure to ever change or improve. The only real alternative was to put a teacher on notice and begin the formal, legal process of remediation and documentation that could lead to dismissal. Because districts do not enter into this action lightly or often—nor should they—few districts have done much to assist teachers. Most teachers who are having difficulties are *marginal*, not *incompetent*. Marginal teachers generally have the capacity to improve their skills. But improvement will usually not occur through that teacher's individual initiative. Marginal teachers can improve—through a focused, supported, and required remediation experience. This second group of typical Track III members can be helped through an assistance program.

Teachers often ask whether being placed in Track III is a prelude to dismissal. No matter how hard a district evaluation committee works to support quality assurance through a professional learning environment, people will always have questions about the motives of a new evaluation system. Districts should not

back away from their commitment to remove teachers who consistently perform below expectations. By design, Track III will involve teachers who, at some point, may be considered or even recommended for dismissal on the basis of incompetence. This will happen because every teacher in the district who may be experiencing some difficulties will first be moved into Track III. Unless a teacher commits some serious transgression that could be judged to be irremediable, the district would not recommend any staff members for dismissal until they had spent time in the district's own professional assistance system.

The design of Track III, however, should have as a goal that almost everyone who is placed in this program will be successful and will be go back to full involvement in Track II, the professional development program. (Issues raised by dismissal, although not really a focus of the new evaluation systems, are briefly discussed later in this chapter to help explain the distinction between dismissal for incompetence and involvement in an assistance program.)

Evaluation committees need to keep staff informed about the positive motives that shape the new assistance programs. Ultimately, people will change their attitudes when the new system is implemented and the staff can see that almost everyone who gets involved with the assistance program benefits professionally and personally.

The Decision for Involvement in Track III

The decision to move a teacher into Track III is the responsibility of the immediate supervisor. As with any form of teacher evaluation, the basis for this decision is the supervisor's professional judgment. The supervisor may form the judgment during the formal/cycled summative evaluation experience or at any time, regardless of whether a formal evaluation has occurred. Supervisors' professional judgments are a recognized and legitimate form of authority within any organization. This is especially true in education because we know of no recognized objective measures of teaching performance, at least none that is within the capacity of local school districts.

To guard against any inappropriate use of supervisory authority, most school districts have in place several checks and balances. These constitutional, statutory, and local contractual protections are safeguards to any misuse of the Track III program. Experience suggests that there are few documented instances of abuse of the assistance program. Nonetheless, local committees need to identify—and clearly communicate to staff—the options that are available if staff members feel that a supervisor has made an inappropriate decision in moving them into the assistance program. If the evaluation committee has built the system to reflect the *supportive* nature of this program, however, most staff members will not object to the presence of or the need for the assistance program.

Supervisors making Track III judgments should hold the teacher's performance against the standards for teaching that the district has adopted as part of the new design. In our experience, teachers expect that any verbal or written notice of being moved into Track III would state the specific standards that, in the judgment of the supervisor, the teacher is not meeting satisfactorily.

In Chapter 4, we raised the issue of discussing the relative importance of the standards. This becomes especially relevant when dealing

with Track III. As with any list of criteria or standards, it is impossible to provide items of equal importance. Using Danielson's (1996) framework as an example, all of the domains, components, and elements are a part of the framework because of their identified effect on teaching and learning. But they are not all equally important to effective teaching. By their inclusion in the framework, the individual statements are a part of the district's vision of what good teaching should involve. Consequently, each item can be seen as a legitimate reason for being placed in Track III. Realistically, however, a supervisor would not use *all* elements as the basis for a Track III decision.

To bring some clarity to this issue, many districts are deciding to identify those items that they deem especially critical. Districts that go through a "weighting of standards" process are providing their administrators and teachers with a set of core standards that every teacher is expected to meet. Failure to satisfactorily meet any of these core expectations automatically triggers the Track III procedures. Figure 10.1 shows a set of weighted standards developed by the Macomb, Illinois, School District. This district, with some slight modifications, adopted Danielson's (1996) framework as the district standards. The local evaluation committee, made up of a representative group of district staff, went through each component and the accompanying elements and identified those that they felt should be specified as core competencies. When the committee introduced the new system to the faculty, they specifically identified and defined these items as required teaching standards for everyone. Using weighted standards does not prevent supervisors from using any other individual

Domain	Competency (with Weighted Items)*
	FIGURE 10.1 **Macomb, Illinois, School District** **The Four Domains for Professional Competency**
Domain 1: Planning and Preparation	*1a. Demonstrating Knowledge of Subject Matter and Pedagogy (the art and science of teaching) *1b. Demonstrating Knowledge of Students *1c. Selecting Instructional Goals *1d. Demonstrating Knowledge of Resources *1e. Designing Coherent Instruction 1f. Assessing Student Learning
Domain 2: The Classroom Environment	*2a. Creating an Environment of Respect and Rapport 2b. Establishing a Culture for Learning *2c. Managing Classroom Procedures *2d. Managing Student Behavior 2c. Organizing Learning Environment
Domain 3: Instruction	3a. Communicating Clearly and Accurately 3b. Using Questioning and Discussion Techniques *3c. Engaging Students in Learning 3d. Providing Feedback to Students *3e. Demonstrating Flexibility and Responsiveness
Domain 4: Professional Responsibilities	4a. Reflecting on Teaching *4b. Maintaining Accurate Records *4c. Communicating with Families *4d. Contributing to the School and District 4e. Growing and Developing Professionally 4f. Showing Professionalism 4g. Utilizing Technology

*Core competencies.

standard for a Track III decision; but it clearly signals that the district will require satisfactory performance in certain areas.

Districts that identify core areas are not trying to move more teachers into the assistance program, but are attempting to assist and motivate teachers who have fallen into the cracks because of poorly designed evaluation systems.

As previously noted, many participants in Track III are teachers who performed poorly in certain important areas because traditional evaluation systems did not include mechanisms for working with marginal teachers. Track III is this mechanism, and the weighted standards are the clear notification of what the district expects of teachers.

Many districts also see this process as a way to encourage or require school administrators to use the assistance program. Because some administrators have traditionally been hesitant to use the assistance program (because they were uncomfortable making the decision, or did not want the added work), the assistance program ended up being used only for incompetent teachers, not the marginal teachers for which it was primarily designed. But in a system with weighted standards—identified and used as automatic triggers into Track III—administrators will likely feel supported in decisions to move particular teachers into the assistance program.

Not every district will feel the need or have the will to go through this process. But every local evaluation committee needs to have the conversation.

The Design of Track III

As with Tracks I and II, evaluation committees should base their decisions on local contexts, past histories, and—particularly with Track III—levels of trust between teachers and administrators. Despite local variations, the design of the assistance program will usually follow a consistent pattern.

To attend to the different levels of performance and the specific situations that problems with certain standards might present, most districts are including as many as three levels of assistance within Track III: awareness, intensive assistance, and disciplinary actions.

Awareness Phase

The first level is often identified as the awareness phase. Districts usually handle this stage in one of two ways. First, some districts encourage administrators to make informal contacts with the teachers with whom the administrators feel there may be a problem in addressing a particular standard. This contact is an opportunity to express the concern, get the teacher's response, set up an observation or some other form of data collection, or give specific suggestions. The goal is to see if the problem can be addressed through this personal interaction between the teacher and the administrator, without formal paperwork or documentation. It is not unlike what normally occurs whenever a supervisor has a concern or a question about some aspect of a teacher's work. This informal intervention might go on for as long as a month or two and, in many cases, would lead to a resolution of the problem. At this point, the teacher would continue to be actively involved in a professional development plan as a part of Track II.

As a second type of awareness activities, some districts recommend this initial contact and attempt at resolution, but require the administrator to make some written documentation of the contact. The intent of the first stage is still to try to resolve the situation through an informal intervention, but often the union or the administration will require some written verification of the nature and purpose of the contact. Figure 10.2 describes a typical assistance program established by a local school district. It requires that the awareness phase include some written documentation, but at a less specific level than is expected in the second or third phases of the program.

In the awareness phase, districts usually establish a time frame to bring some closure to this first stage. Normally, one of three decisions is made at the conclusion of the established time:

FIGURE 10.2
Macomb, Illinois, School District
Plan III: Specific Staff Development

Awareness Phase

1. The administrator or the teacher identifies a concern in writing. (Identification of Concern Form)

2. The administrator and the teacher set up a specific time to collaborate and attempt to resolve the concern.

3. At the conclusion of the Awareness Phase, the administrator will review the progress and will make one of the following recommendations:

- The teacher remains in Plan II, Professional Growth.
- In the event the concern is not resolved or is a disciplinary issue, the teacher is placed into either the Assistance or Disciplinary Phase. (Final Summary Form)

At this point, the teacher will be advised by the principal to discuss the situation with the association President or designated representative. The teacher or the administrator may request other representation in all subsequent meetings regarding the concern.

Assistance Phase

1. Review the recommendations from the Awareness Phase.

2. A specific plan will be developed which includes: (Plan of Assistance Form)

- Growth-promoting goals that are specific, measurable, action oriented, realistic, and time bound (S.M.A.R.T.).
- Strategies for resolution of the concern.
- Time lines.
- Indicators of progress.
- Resources and support needed.

3. The administrator and the teacher set up a specific time to review what progress has been made. (Plan of Assistance Progress Form)

4. One of the following recommendations will be made upon reviewing the teacher's progress: (Final Summary Form)

- The concern is resolved and the teacher is returned to the Professional Growth Plan.
- The teacher remains in the Assistance Phase with revised goals and time lines.

- The concern is not resolved and the teacher is moved into the Disciplinary Phase.

Note: Data obtained during the Assistance Phase may not be used in further action against the teacher. An exception would be an event or specific data that initiates a move from the Awareness Phase or the Assistance Phase into the Disciplinary Phase.

Disciplinary Phase

1. The teacher may be placed in the Disciplinary Phase because of, but not limited to:

- Not meeting the Standards for Effective Teaching after being in the Assistance Phase.
- Insubordination.
- Specific policy or rule violation(s).

2. The Disciplinary Phase begins with a meeting between the administrator, teacher, and association President or designated representative. Other resource people may be involved, i.e., central office administrator(s) or a "uniserve" representative (a union designation for a regional office).

3. The administrator will identify in writing the specific Standard(s), rule, or policy in violation. (Disciplinary Phase) The teacher will be given an opportunity to respond. Following the discussion, the administrator will indicate the next steps to be taken, such as:

- A specific remedial plan with time line.
- Placement of the teacher on paid administrative leave.
- Requirement of specific training or evaluation by a professional.
- Recommendation for nonrenewal of contract.
- Recommendation for tenure review by the Superintendent and Board of Education.

4. This Disciplinary Phase only addresses ongoing performance concerns not corrected by the teacher under either the Awareness Phase or the Assistance Phase. The Disciplinary Phase is not intended as a restriction on the district's right to take appropriate disciplinary action for teacher misconduct without prior resort to either an Awareness Phase or an Assistance Phase.

1. The teacher has resolved the problem or concern and continues working on her professional development plan.

2. The teacher or the administrator, or both, feel that continuing to work at this stage will benefit the teacher so the time within the awareness phase is extended.

3. The administrator determines that the teacher is not making satisfactory progress at this level and begins the process of moving the teacher to the second stage, assistance.

Assistance Phase

The second stage commonly has titles such as intensive assistance, professional support, or professional assistance. This stage begins a more specific and intensive involvement between the teacher and the administrator or between the teacher and an assistance team. A key component of this more intensive stage is the development of an action plan or improvement plan. Conley (1987) provides the following recommendations for the action plan:

- Identify each criterion needing improvement.
- State the criterion as a goal for the activity.
- State behaviors that must be demonstrated at the end of the plan.
- State specific interventions that will be used to help produce the desired behavior.
- State how behavior changes will be documented.

Figure 10.2 offers an example of second-stage procedures that generally follow these recommendations. Some districts add a wrinkle by including other professionals in this stage of assistance. Many believe that the administrator who has worked with the teacher through the awareness phase, and who has made the decision to take the process to a more intense level, may not be the best person to continue to take the lead in providing assistance to the teacher. At this point, it may be desirable to identify a group of people with special expertise and knowledge who may be able to provide the support and direction that will allow and encourage the teacher to improve his or her performance. The make-up of the team will vary; but in most cases, it will consist of a group of teachers, a mixed group of teachers and an administrator, or a group of all administrators, but not including the primary evaluator. The teacher in the assistance program and the responsible administrator would help to identify the group. The team would work with the teacher on the plan of action, and in some cases, with the consent of the administrator, actually develop the action plan with the teacher. The team, whether it is all teachers, all administrators, or a mixed group, would not be involved in making the summative decision regarding whether the teacher has met the desired outcome: That role would remain with the responsible administrator. Figure 10.3 shows an example of the use of a team, including explanations of the role of the team, the role of the administrator, and the expectations for the staff member who is involved in Track III.

Many districts require that teachers in this phase of assistance stop all involvement in their professional development plan in Track II and devote all their energy to work on the identified problems. Other districts have left this decision to the teacher and the administrator. If the teacher is involved in a team plan, a peer coaching activity, or some other option that involves collaboration, the teacher and administrator may decide that the teacher should stay with the other project while

FIGURE 10.3
Macomb, Illinois, School District
Track III: Staff Assistance Program

Tracks I and II of the Appraisal Process for instructional staff are designed to recognize and improve good teaching. The vast majority of the staff will be well served by this process. For those few staff members who have not demonstrated satisfactory performance on the Professional Performance Expectations, a more directive and intensive system of support is necessary.

Purposes

- To demonstrate the commitment of the District to the ongoing growth and development of all staff.
- To improve the performance of staff members who have been identified by their administrators as needing assistance in meeting Professional Performance Expectations.
- To implement a process which is positive and should assist in professional growth.

Level A: Skill Assistance

Procedures

When an administrator's observation and/or evaluation (utilizing the Professional Performance Expectation form in Track I) of any staff member indicates a performance problem, the supervisor may develop an individualized improvement program. This program will focus on specific areas of the Professional Performance Expectations and will most frequently take the form of the formal observation process as outlined in Track I. Other forms of data collection or assistance may be designed by the supervisor with input of the individual staff member. At any time during this appraisal cycle, the supervisor could make one of the following recommendations:

1. Move the staff member into Professional Growth Track II.

2. Retain staff member in Staff Assistance Track III, Level A. (The staff member may continue team-level work in Track II).

3. Move the staff member into Staff Assistance Track III, Level B, Intensive Assistance.

Level B: Intensive Assistance

When an administrator's observation and/or evaluation of any staff member indicates a significant level of unsatisfactory performance on the District Professional Performance Expectations, a recommendation is made to the Director of Personnel for intensive assistance. Documentation (including observations utilizing the Professional Performance Expectation form in Track I) supporting the unsatisfactory performance must accompany the request.

The administrator's recommendation for an Intensive Assistance team will be reviewed by the Director of Personnel to verify that progressive assistance has occurred, to substantiate that the teacher has had sufficient notification in writing that his/her performance does not meet Professional Performance Expectations, and to determine if adequate data are present to enable an Intensive Assistance team to be effective.

If the administrator's recommendation for Intensive Assistance is approved by the Director of Personnel, the administrator and the Director of Personnel will meet with the staff member whose performance is unsatisfactory and introduce the concept of Intensive Assistance.

The Director of Personnel will assign members to the District team who have experience or expertise in the performance area which is in need of improvement. However, the teachers asked will have the right to decline the assignment. Typically, the team will be made up of the following members:

A. One member responsible for expertise in instructional strategy.

B. One member responsible for expertise in the subject area, grade level or general curriculum.

C. One teacher—the staff member will submit the names of three teachers they would like to work with during this process. The Director of Personnel will select one of these three to be a team member.

D. Other members as deemed appropriate by the Director of Personnel. At least one member of the team must be an administrator.

(continued)

FIGURE 10.3
(continued)

The Intensive Assistance team will work with the Director of Personnel to plan the observation and conference schedule.

The Director of Personnel and the Intensive Assistance team will meet with the original building administrator to introduce the team members, to outline the process, and to inform the administrator of the time schedule. At this time, the staff member's evaluations will be reviewed and the administrator will inform team members of previous and current attempts at remediation.

The Intensive Assistance team will met with the staff member to review the role of the team, to verify the observation and conference schedule, and to receive input from the staff member.

The length of service of the Intensive Assistance team will vary, depending on the needs of the staff member. It may not exceed one calendar year.

Role of the Team

The role of the Intensive Assistance team is to use data and information provided by the administrator to develop a planned approach to help the staff member meet Professional Performance Expectations. The plan will usually include, but is not limited to, direct observation of teaching or other activities, conferencing with the staff member, peer coaching, mentoring and follow-up activities. The plan may include any number of additional strategies designed to assist the instructional process.

A log of meetings held with the staff member will be maintained by each member of the Intensive Assistance team. The log will be given to the Director of Personnel when the process is completed. Team members will use the following guidelines in communicating with the staff member; suggestions for improvement will be provided and multiple options presented. Comments will relate to specific situations, i.e., your motivational techniques worked well with your first group today. General statements, such as, "You are doing better at motivating students," will be avoided.

Strict confidentiality will be maintained. No reference will be made to the name of the staff member or the building where the team is meeting. Team members will communicate regularly with the Director of Personnel to report observations

conferences and progress. Team members' observations and conferences are not presented in writing, are not reported to the building administrator, and do not become part of the staff member's evaluation.

Role of the Administrator

A staff member who is receiving intensive assistance will be placed on an appraisal cycle as outlined in Track I. The building administrator continues to be the evaluator of the staff member. The Director of Personnel is responsible to maintain communication between the teacher and the building administrator. The Intensive Assistance process does not delay or replace the normal supervision and evaluation process. After Intensive Assistance has ended, the building administrator completes an evaluation and makes one of the following recommendations to the Director of Personnel:

1. To return the staff member to Track II, or

2. To recommend the continuation of the Intensive Assistance Program with a different team, or

3. To turn over to the Director of Personnel for further action as per negotiated agreement.

At the discretion of the Director, an administrator or staff member may request a second evaluator to conduct additional observation(s) and conference(s). Members of the Intensive Assistance team will not be used as second evaluators. Additional evaluations/ observations may be conducted by the administrator at any time.

Responsibilities of the Staff Member Placed on Track III

1. To ask for clarifications from the Intensive Assistance team, the Director of Personnel and the building administrator.

2. To be responsible for total anecdotal notes during the process, if desired.

3. To request, if desired, a Teacher's Association representative to be present with him/her during Intensive Assistance team meetings.

4. To be open and flexible in implementing different and/or refined strategies in improving his/her Professional Performance Expectations.

5. To be responsible in meeting deadlines, appointments, scheduled observations, and other time lines.

involved in Track III. In this way, the team's progress is not hampered, and the teacher's involvement in the assistance program is not so obvious to others. This point should be discussed by the committee as they design this track.

The plan presented in Figure 10.2 has an interesting note at the end of the assistance phase:

> Data obtained during the Assistance Phase may not be used in further action against the teacher. An exception would be an event or specific data that initiate a move from the Awareness Phase or the Assistance Phase into the Disciplinary Phase.

Several districts are including similar statements at the end of the second stage in their assistance program. As a way to support the spirit of assistance that is behind the establishment of Track III, districts are willing to concede that data or information gathered in the awareness or professional support stages will *not* be used in any further action against the teacher. This statement is a gesture that supports the professional nature of the new Track III designs and the commitment to the spirit of assistance. The assumption is that if a supervisor moves a teacher into the more serious third stage of Track III, the district will need to apply more legal rules of documentation. This process would be the source of evidence for use in a possible dismissal case, and the earlier work done in Phases 1 and 2 of Track III are neither necessary nor helpful. The inclusion of this type of statement may be helpful in lowering the teacher anxiety produced by a district developing its first formal remediation program as a part of a new evaluation system. This idea

will not be necessary in every situation, but should be discussed by the evaluation committee.

When the teacher has reached the established time frame in the second stage of Track III, the responsible administrator will again be faced with three possible actions:

1. The teacher has met or implemented the established goal or the desired behavior, is moved fully back into Track II, and continues working on the professional development plan.

2. The teacher has not met or reached the desired or established outcome of the Phase 2 action plan, but the teacher is committed to working toward meeting the plan and has made progress. In this case, the teacher and supervisor establish a new time line and interventions; and the teacher continues work within Phase 2.

3. The teacher has not met the goals of the plan, teacher commitment is questionable, and the supervisor has noted no progress. In this case, the recommendation is to move to the next, and most serious level.

Disciplinary Phase

This next level may be seen as the third stage in the assistance program (see Figure 10.2) or may be the movement, with proper notification, of the teacher into a legal process mandated by the state or by the local negotiated contract (see Figure 10.3).

Meeting Legal Requirements. If the system has been designed properly and a spirit of professional assistance is guiding the interventions and the relationships within this track, then most staff who have been placed in the assistance program will never reach this third stage. The sample assistance plan presented in Figure

10.2 uses this third stage as a more formal, legalized intervention that *may* lead to dismissal. In most cases, movement to this third stage starts with a notice to the teacher association that the teacher has been moved to this phase. As well, the supervisor may inform the teacher that she may contact the association and ask for their assistance. This suggested or required action is an example of the more serious nature of this phase. The design of this stage will closely resemble the required activities in the earlier stages. The major difference is that everything is now proceeding at a more urgent pace and with a more serious tone.

In Case of Dismissal: Guidelines for Districts. The experience of those districts that view their teacher evaluation designs as successful suggests that their Track III programs have been helpful. Unfortunately, not all remediation efforts have a happy ending. In some cases, the teacher will either be unwilling or unable to meet the district's standards. It is not the intent of Track III to increase the likelihood of teacher dismissals on the basis of incompetency. This has not been the case in districts who have designed new remediation programs. But it is a reality that districts must address.

Here are some guidelines that can serve to help both districts and teachers understand the requirements and the protections that are a part of making an incompetency case against a tenured teacher:

1. The district must define as clearly as possible the nature and the pattern of the teacher's incompetence.

2. The district must establish a record of factual evidence to support the claim of a continuing pattern of the teacher's incompetence.

3. The district should consult with its attorney to determine if evidence gathered is sufficient to sustain a charge of incompetency in view of applicable state legal standards.

4. The district should consider explanations of facts that may be used in the teacher's defense, such as differences in educational philosophy, difficult working conditions, prejudice against the teacher, and failure to allow adequate opportunity for remediation.

5. The district should consider the potential effect of a teacher's dismissal on staff morale, including positive effects of establishing high teacher performance standards and negative effects resulting from misunderstanding the grounds for dismissal.

6. The district must ensure that adequate warning of undesirable behavior or incompetency has been given through official remediation notices.

7. The district must ensure that desired behavior and practices are substantially related to reasonable expectations in teacher performance.

8. The district must ensure that all investigation efforts and evidence gathering has been conduced fairly and objectively.

9. The district must ensure that standards of behavior and teaching practice have been applied fairly and without prejudice.

10. The district must be convinced of the seriousness of the charges against the teacher and be prepared to bear the burden of proof in making its case.

The move to a recommendation for possible dismissal that would occur at the end of the Track III process or in the third stage of Track III does represent the least desirable outcome of evaluation. Districts and schools, however, must decide how to protect students and the education profession from the continuing presence of a bad teacher. But local evaluation committees, the administrative staff, and the teachers must remember that dealing with "bad" teachers is a small fraction of evaluation activity, at best.

☞ ☞ ☞

In building the new evaluation systems described in this book, districts have displayed this vision: Quality assurance based on a clearly established set of teaching standards can be accomplished within an environment that promotes and encourages professional learning. Forty years of study regarding teacher evaluation indicates that teachers and administrators recognize the importance and the necessity for staff evaluation. The problem for both groups has been with the way schools have done it in the past. This book offers a view of how it should be done.

Epilogue

Karen and Charles (our teacher and principal from the Prologue) are trapped in a meaningless ritual of activity called "evaluation." They go through the motions of conducting conferences and observations, discussing teaching, and evaluating performance. They know, on some level, that the process they are using does not satisfy either of the essential purposes of evaluation—ensuring quality in teaching and promoting professional learning.

As we have demonstrated in this book, however, it is possible to employ evaluation procedures that engage both teachers and administrators in a professional dialogue about students, their learning, and teaching. This can be accomplished without radically restructuring the entire school district, spending huge amounts of money, or engaging in other kinds of efforts often demanded by transforming ideas. Instead, the educators involved simply must think differently about an activity—teacher evaluation—in which they are already engaged and which is required by law.

Using such an approach, for example, Karen could have conducted a self-assessment; she could have identified areas in which she wanted to concentrate (such as the English-language learners in her classroom, or the new math or writing programs). She and Charles could have developed a plan to address those issues, and Karen could have worked with colleagues in pursuing her plan. Karen and Charles's conversations could have been about genuine instructional matters, and both would have grown professionally through the experience.

This approach would involve Karen in an active role, through self-assessment, assembling items for a portfolio, and professional conversation. Even if Charles makes the final judgment, Karen is more actively engaged in the process, offering interpretations for classroom events, providing rationales for instructional decisions, and offering evidence of nonclassroom aspects of her responsibilities (such as samples of letters sent to parents of her non-English speaking students). Further, Karen would have been invited to question Charles's judgments, offer additional evidence of her skill, or provide alternate interpretations of the same information. This would not constitute insubordination—Charles, after all, is making the final judgment—but it would provide a forum for genuine professional conversation. And as a by-product of the conversation, Charles would be likely to learn as well.

Appendixes: Evaluation Case Studies

Many school districts have implemented teacher evaluation systems using the principles identified in this book. Two of them, in Addison, Illinois, and in Newport News, Virginia, are described more fully here. Both of these systems employ a differentiated approach, with different procedures for novice and experienced teachers. They also engage teachers actively in the evaluation process, thereby ensuring that they will experience professional growth as a result of the effort.

Appendix A contains a description of the evaluation system in place in Addison, Illinois. Many of the forms used in that system are included in the description of the recommended procedures in Chapters 8–10.

Appendix B contains a summary of the evaluation system in use in Newport News, Virginia, and a sampling of the forms used.

Other School Districts with Three-Track Systems

Other examples of three-track models that focus on quality assurance and professional development can be obtained by contacting the following school districts:

West Morris Regional High School District
Four Bridges Road
Chester, NJ 07930

Maine School Administrative District #51
Cumberland-North Yarmouth
P.O. Box 6A
Cumberland, ME 04021

East Grand Rapids School District
2915 Hall Street SE
East Grand Rapids, MI 49506

Unionville-Chadds Ford School District
740 Unionville Road
Kennett Square, PA 19348

Bartholomew Consolidated School Corporation
2650 Home Avenue
Columbus, IN 47201

Dubuque Community Schools
2300 Chaney Road
Dubuque, IA 52001-3095

Greenwood Public Schools
440 West Gary
Greenwood, AR 72936

Grosse Ile Township Schools
23270 East River
Grosse Ile, MI 48138

Appendix A
Addison, Illinois, Public Schools

A Summary of Addison's Professional Appraisal System

Addison School District #4
222 N. Kennedy Dr.
Addison, IL 60101
(630) 458-2500
Dr. Larry Weck, Superintendent

The Addison system is an excellent example of a three-track system. The system is driven by a philosophy developed by the joint teacher-administrator evaluation committee.

Statement of Philosophy

Addison School District 4 is committed to providing the best educational program for its students. To this end, it supports a professional appraisal system that focuses on excellence. The system is based on teachers and administrators working together in the process of continual improvement of teaching and learning.

We believe . . .

- All staff members recognize the benefits of professional development to achieve the goals of the school and district.
- All staff members are committed to continual improvement of professional performance.

- Appraisal of performance is based on a cooperative spirit, open communication, and joint responsibility.
- Appraisal of performance is positive in nature and intent. It recognizes strengths and provides a means for support and improvement.
- Appraisal of performance is designed to promote excellence in teaching and learning.

The committee identified Danielson's (1996) framework for teaching as the best representation of what the district believed to be the core standards for performance. Once the framework was identified and plans for providing staff development that focused on the Danielson domains, elements, and expectations to the staff were developed, the committee began the work of designing each of the three tracks.

The initial description of the components of each track was developed by subcommittees. The drafts were then presented to the whole group for discussion and revision. The process of selecting the committee, developing the guiding philosophy, identifying the core standards, designing the components of each track, and getting the new system introduced to the faculty, was a year-long process.

The major elements of each track were as follows.

Pre-Tenured Teacher—Track I

Illinois has a four-year probation period for new teachers. Addison determined that the first two years would be more intensive and that a serious discussion would be made at that point before renewing for the third year. Consequently, they dropped some of the required activities in years 3 and 4 to lessen the time commitment on their administrators. They identified formal observations, required artifact collection, and required journal writing as the activities that best represented the type of information they wanted to collect to enable them to make rational personnel decisions while still promoting professional learning. These Track I procedures were supported by an existing induction program, a beginning teacher mentor program, and a series of required staff development programs.

Professional Growth Plan—Track II

Addison chose to appraise their tenured staff through the continuous feedback gained through the daily interactions, visits, and stakeholder feedback that is a natural part of the life of a school. There are no required observations or cycled summative evaluations of the tenured teachers. Participation in Track II is seen as a recognition of a staff member's meeting of the core standards.

This district (a K–8 district with a fully articulated middle school) put a heavy emphasis on teams of staff writing and implementing professional development plans (strongly encouraged, but not required). Plans may be set for one, two, or three years, but there is a clear preference for multiyear plans.

Professional Assistance Plan—Track III

The Addison Track III closely follows the basic recommendations for an assistance program. The Awareness phase is an opportunity for the principal to contact a teacher regarding a concern and begin a series of conversations, observations, and assistance strategies. If progress is not occurring, then the teacher is moved to the more intensive and directed support phase. If satisfactory progress does not occur within the support phase, the administrator, with district approval, may move the staff member to the state remediation plan. The statutory state process contains a series of legally mandated notification requirements, strict requirements for documentation of teacher performance, and the satisfying of a set of due process procedures that can support a dismissal on the basis of incompetence. (Figures A1 (p. 134), for nontenured teachers, and A2 (p. 135), for tenured teachers, show the three-track system in Addison.)

FIGURE A1
Pretenured Appraisal System

Addison School District 4
Professional Appraisal System
Pretenured Staff Members

Year 1:

Formal Observations (3)
Pre- and post-conferences
Post-observation form by administrator
Observation reflection form by staff member

Artifact Collection
Documentation and support of professional competencies and growth

Journal
Reflective writing by staff member

Summative Review
Written appraisal by administrator

Year 2, 3 and 4:

Formal Observations (2)
Pre- and post-conferences
Pre-observation form by staff member
Post-observation form by administrator
Observation reflection form by staff member

Artifact Collection
Documentation and support of professional growth

Journal
Reflective writing by staff member
Required in years 1 and 2, optional in years 3 and 4

Summative Review
Written appraisal by administrator

FIGURE A2
Tenured Appraisal System
Addison School District 4 **Professional Appraisal System** **Tenured Staff Members**

Professional Growth Plan

Part 1: Ongoing appraisal

Informal

Varied settings

Based on professional competencies

Part 2: Professional Development

Based on specific need

Directed toward improvement of student learning

Individually determined

Collaboratively developed

Collaboratively implemented

Collaboratively assessed

Professional Assistance Plan

Based on specific need

Directed toward improvement of professional competencies

Initiated by teacher or administrator

Collaboratively developed, implemented

Phase 1: Awareness

Short term, quick progress, concerns resolved

Phase 2: Support

Specific action plan, time line for progress

State of Illinois Remediation Plan

Appendix B
Newport News, Virginia, Public Schools

Overview of Teacher Evaluation System

Newport News, Virginia, Public Schools
12465 Warwick boulevard
Newport News, VA 23606-6130

Newport News Public Schools is an urban district in Virginia with 45 schools serving 32,000 students in grades preK–12. The development of their Teacher Performance Assessment Handbook involved the commitment of hundreds of teachers, school and district-level administrators, and school board members. The design initiative began with a committee of volunteers who were supported by a consultant. Initially five schools field-tested and revised draft documents for two years. Due to insufficient teacher ownership, the school board approved an additional year for an expanded field-test that involved all grade levels. By faculty votes of 90 percent or more, 20 schools opted into the third year of field-testing.

It was at this point that performance scales and the concepts of evidence from *Enhancing Professional Practice: A Framework for Teaching* (Danielson, 1996) were incorporated with Charlotte Danielson's support and guidance. Formative and summative assessment processes were differentiated as distinct yet critical assessment cycles. After this third year of field-testing and more refinement, the procedures

and documents in the process had sufficient teacher ownership to be approved by the district school board. Throughout these four years, the staff development department organized summer lead team conferences and quarterly dialogues in the areas of effective teaching, leading change, and sharing "what works" and "how this could be better." Members of lead teams—teachers and administrators—assumed the responsibility for scheduling and leading customized staff development sessions at their own schools.

The Newport News evaluation system is structured as a differentiated system, with somewhat different procedures required for probationary teachers and for teachers under continuing contract.

Probationary Teachers. All probationary teachers are engaged in the summative evaluation process each year until they receive a continuing contract, typically after three years' teaching in Newport News.

Continuing Contract Teachers. Every fourth year (or when it is deemed necessary by an administrator), teachers under continuing contract engage in a summative evaluation process, in which administrators make judgments about teachers' performance. During the other three years of the cycle, teachers engage in a formative process, under the direction of the teacher, in which they conduct a self-assessment, set growth goals, and, with colleagues in a support team, engage in professional growth activities.

The following sections describe the summative and formative procedures, and some of the instruments and forms used.

The Formative Process

Those continuing contract teachers not involved in summative evaluation participate in the formative process each year. This process composes the heart of the district's approach to professional development: self-directed, collegial, and results-based. Offerings from the staff development office, as well as training opportunities from other sources, may be incorporated into individual growth plans and used to support the achievement of teachers' goals.

In the formative process, each teacher conducts a self-assessment and selects, with an administrator, suitable goals for focus. The teacher then joins a support team, develops a growth plan, and implements that plan. The process is directed by the teacher, and results in documentation of enhanced skill which is then available for submission during the summative evaluation process.

Some of the forms used in this process are shown in Figures B1 through B5.

The Summative Process

All probationary teachers and continuing contract teachers every fourth year (or more frequently if it is deemed necessary by an administrator) participate in a summative evaluation process. This process ensures that all Newport News teachers uphold the high standards of practice demanded by high standards for student learning, and comprises the district's method of ensuring that all students have the benefit of instruction at a high level of proficiency.

In the summative process, these steps are followed:

- Teacher completes self-assessment.
- Teacher and administrator conduct the initial summative conference (by November 1).
- Administrator conducts two formal observations of the teacher, consisting of a pre-observation conference, an observation, and a post-observation conference. These observations are completed by February 1.
- Teacher collects evidence of his or her practice, including the Instructional Unit and unit artifacts, the Family Contact Log, and the Professional Development/ School, District, and Community Contributions Log.
- Teacher and administrator hold a conference to review the teacher's documentation. Administrator completes the summative evaluation, assessing the teacher's performance.

Plan of Action (Intervention for Less-Than-Satisfactory Teacher Performance)

In the event that a teacher's performance is less than satisfactory according to any stated performance expectation, the administrator and the teacher collaboratively develop a Plan of Action to address the deficiencies in performance. The Plan of Action will include the following elements:

- A time line for plan implementation (in accordance with the time line for contract renewal).
- Persons responsible for each step of the plan.

- Assistance to be provided by the principal or others.
- Assessment criteria and procedures.
- Schedule for interim conferences to discuss the status of the plan implementation.
- Signatures of the teacher and the administrator.

The Newport News process now enjoys the commitment and respect of educators from across the district. The experience of designing and implementing an effective teacher performance assessment, however, was found to take districtwide commitment of time, investment of human and fiscal resources, and the involvement of a large percentage of teachers and administrators. Underlying all this collaborative work was the unifying belief that teachers are leaders and designers of knowledge work for their students and for themselves.

The forms used in the process are shown in Figures B6 through B15 (pp. 139–53).

FIGURE B1
Self-Assessment Worksheet I

Carefully reflect on your teaching performance in all four domains. Complete the Self-Assessment by using the tables showing levels of performance. Prepare to discuss your performance in all domains during the goal-setting conference with your administrator.

Key: U. . . . Unsatisfactory   B. . . . Basic   P. . . . Proficient   D. . . . Distinguished

Domain 1: Designing Knowledge Work	U	B	P	D
1a. Demonstrating Knowledge of Content and Pedagogy				
1b. Demonstrating Knowledge of Students				
1c. Selecting Instructional Goals				
1d. Demonstrating Knowledge of Resources				
1e. Designing Coherent Instruction				
1f. Assessing Student Learning Through Student-Generated Products				
Domain 2: Organizing the Environment for Knowledge Work				
2a. Creating an Environment of Respect and Rapport				
2b. Establishing a Culture for Learning by Supporting of Beliefs, Vision, and Mission of Newport News Public Schools				
2c. Managing Classroom Procedures				
2d. Managing Student Behavior				
2e. Managing Physical Space				
Domain 3: Facilitating Knowledge Work				
3a. Communicating Clearly and Accurately				
3b. Using Questioning and Discussion Techniques				
3c. Engaging Students in the Work				
3d. Affirming the Performance of Students				
3e. Demonstrating Flexibility and Responsiveness Through Monitoring and Modifying the Work				
Domain 4: Professional and Leadership Responsibilities				
4a. Reflecting on Teaching				
4b. Maintaining Accurate Records				
4c. Communicating with Families				
4d. Contributing Leadership to the School and Division				
4e. Growing and Developing Professionally				
4f. Showing Professionalism				

FIGURE B2		
Self-Assessment Worksheet II		
Noted Areas of Strength	**Possible Areas for Growth**	**Suggested Growth Goals**

FIGURE B3			
Formative Assessment: Self-Directed Professional Growth Plan			

Name _____School Year _____

Support Team Members_____

Growth Goal(s)

The goal(s) addresses components in (check all that apply)
❑ Domain 1   ❑ Domain 2   ❑ Domain 3   ❑ Domain 4

Activities and Steps to Be Taken	**Persons/Resources Needed**	**Documentation**	**Time Line and Deadlines**

FIGURE B4
Formative Support Team Meeting Log

Complete one form per support team for each meeting held. Submit a copy to the administrator/designee.

Meeting Date_____Time _____Place _____

Members Present _____

_____

_____

Topics Discussed

Administrative Support, Feedback, Resources, and Staff Development Needed

Next Meeting Date _____Time _____Place _____

Submitted by _____Date _____

FIGURE B5
Formative Assessment Summary

To be completed by the teacher and shared with Formative Support Team before the last contract day. A copy should also be filed with the administrator/designee before the last contract day.

Name _____ School Year _____

Support Team Members   _____   _____

                                                 _____   _____

                                                 _____   _____

Type of Support Team   ❑ Coach-Advisee   ❑ Collegial Friends   ❑ School-Division Cohort

Describe the professional growth activities in which you participated this year to achieve your growth goal. (Attach additional pages as necessary.)

What results were achieved through these activities?

How did you use your support team to achieve these results?

How did you contribute to your support team members' professional growth?

Other comments or reflections

Teacher's Signature _____ Date _____

Note: When you use this form, allow plenty of space for responses, preferably on two pages.

Figure B6 Summative Assessment: Self-Assessment Worksheet 2				
Carefully reflect on your teaching performance in all four domains and complete the Self-Assessment. Prepare to discuss your performance in all domains during the initial Summative Conference with your assessor prior to November 1. Key: U. . . . Unsatisfactory B. . . . Basic P. . . . Proficient D. . . . Distinguished				
Domain 1: Designing Knowledge Work	**U**	**B**	**P**	**D**
1a. Demonstrating Knowledge of Content and Pedagogy				
1b. Demonstrating Knowledge of Students				
1c. Selecting Instructional Goals				
1d. Demonstrating Knowledge of Resources				
1e. Designing Coherent Instruction				
1f. Assessing Student Learning Through Student-Generated Products				
Domain 2: Organizing the Environment for Knowledge Work				
2a. Creating an Environment of Respect and Rapport				
2b. Establishing a Culture for Learning by Supporting of Beliefs, Vision, and Mission of Newport News Public Schools				
2c. Managing Classroom Procedures				
2d. Managing Student Behavior				
2e. Managing Physical Space				
Domain 3: Facilitating Knowledge Work				
3a. Communicating Clearly and Accurately				
3b. Using Questioning and Discussion Techniques				
3c. Engaging Students in the Work				
3d. Affirming the Performance of Students				
3e. Demonstrating Flexibility and Responsiveness Through Monitoring and Modifying the Work				
Domain 4: Professional and Leadership Responsibilities				
4a. Reflecting on Teaching				
4b. Maintaining Accurate Records				
4c. Communicating with Families				
4d. Contributing Leadership to the School and Division				
4e. Growing and Developing Professionally				
4f. Showing Professionalism				

FIGURE B7
Summative Assessment: Self-Assessment Summary (Optional)

This form may be used as needed to make notes in preparation for the Initial Summative Conference with the assessor.

Domain 1	Domain 2	Domain 3	Domain 4

FIGURE B8
Agenda for Initial Summative Conference

This information is to be provided by the teacher and discussed with the assessor by November I of the Summative Assessment year.

Summative Self-Assessment

Following completion of your Summative Self-Assessment, discuss your performance in each of the four domains.

Knowledge of Students (Evidence of Domain 1)

State the techniques you use to become knowledgeable about your students:

Briefly describe the students in your class including the cultural composition, ethnic background or heritage, those with special needs, and those with limited English proficiency.

Briefly describe the background knowledge and skills of your students.

Classroom Management Procedures (Evidence of Domain 2)

State the classroom rules, procedures, and expectations for student behavior in your classroom.

(Optional evidence could include classroom rules chart, parent letter, class schedule(s), substitute teacher file, etc.)

Describe how these practices were established.

Describe what, if anything, an observer should know about the learning environment which may impact your students' learning.

State the reason(s) for your **room arrangement.**

FIGURE B9
Summative Support Team Review of Evidence

These questions are to be used by Summative Support Teams when providing guidance to members on evidence gathering. These questions are to be used as discussion guides only.

Tell us more about this artifact (work plan, unit, student work, etc.).

For which domain do you think it provides evidence? Why?

Is there a particular component of the domain that you think it best represents?
If so, which component?

What makes this a quality piece of evidence?

What level on the performance tables do you think this evidence portrays?

Why?

What concerns, if any, do you have about submitting this piece of evidence?

If you decide not to use this particular artifact, what else could you use?

Are you considering other pieces that may document the same domain or component?

FIGURE B10
Agenda for Summative Assessment: Pre-observation Conference

(Evidence of Domain 1)

This information is to be provided by the teacher in conference with the assessor prior to each formal classroom observation.

Plan for a Single Lesson

State your goals for the lesson. What do you expect the students to learn?

How do these goals . . .

- reflect the needs of your students?
- reflect your SOL's and curriculum as a whole?
- relate to other content areas?

Explain how your work plan incorporates the **design qualities** to engage your students in the work.

- What will you do?
- What will your students do?
- How much time will be used?

Explain the **difficulties** students typically experience in this area.

- How do you plan to anticipate those difficulties, enabling your students to persist with the work?

State the **instructional materials or other resources** you will use.

- What additional resources, if any, are available through the school or in the larger community that could be used to facilitate your students' learning of this topic/concept?

Explain how you plan to **assess** student achievement of the goals. (Test, performance tasks, scoring guides, rubrics can be used as evidence.)

- What procedures will you use?
- What products will the students produce?

Describe the **accommodations** in your work plan that address the special needs of your students and the diverse population of your class.

Explain anything else the observer should know about your class or your classroom procedures.

If the administrator does not observe this specific lesson, the teacher is not expected to repeat the formal pre-observation conference.

FIGURE B11
Agenda for Summative Assessment: Post-observation Conference

(Evidence of Domain 4)

This information is to be provided by the teacher during the Post-observation Conference. The Post-observation Conference is to be scheduled at least 24 hours after the classroom observation.

As I reflect on the lesson, were the students productively engaged in the work?
How do I know?

Did the students learn what I expected them to learn? Were the instructional goals met?
How do I know?
If I don't know at this point, when will I know? How will I know?

Did I alter my goals or my work plan as I taught this lesson?
Why? How?

If I had the opportunity to teach this lesson again to the same group of students, what would I do differently? Why?

FIGURE B12
School, Division, and Community Contributions Log

This information is to be maintained by the teacher during the Summative Assessment year and submitted to the assessor prior to June 1 in preparation for the Final Summative Conference. This form or its equivalent may be used.

Name _____ Grade/Subject _____ School Year _____

Date	Activity: Workshops, Conferences, Committee Meetings, Open House	Benefits Derived or Contributions Made	Notes

FIGURE B13
Summative Assessment Family Contact Log

This information is to be maintained by the teacher during the Summative Assessment year and submitted to the assessor prior to June 1 in preparation for the Final Summative Conference. This form or its equivalent may be used.

Name _____ Grade/Subject _____ School Year _____

Date	Student Name	Person Contacted	Type of Contact	Reason or Purpose	Notes

FIGURE B14
Instructional Unit and Unit Artifacts for Summative Assessment

The teacher is to provide an instructional unit of at least one week in length, artifacts from that unit, and the following information prior to June 1. This evidence is submitted in preparation for the Final Summative Conference.

Name _____Grade/Subject Taught _____

Grade/Subject of the
Unit and Artifacts_____Dates of the Unit _____

Unit Concept/Topic _____

_____

Objectives/Goals for the Assignment/Student Artifacts Attached:

Attach a copy of a unit you have used in your classroom this year. The unit can be in any format you wish and taken from any point during the year.

Attach an activity or assignment directions that engaged students in authentic work related to the concept or topic cited above. (e.g. project guidelines, problem(s) to solve, homework assignment, center activity)

Provide some evidence of student learning. This should reflect the full range of student achievement levels in your class and should include feedback you provided to your students on their work. (e.g. samples of student work, photographs, audio or video tapes)

Be prepared to reflect on the artifacts and the unit in your Final Summative Conference.

FIGURE B15
Agenda for Final Summative Conference

Instructional Unit and Artifact(s) from the Unit

(Evidence of domains 1 and 4)

Discuss how this unit was developed. In your discussion:

- Explain **why** the content of this unit was chosen and how the goals were determined.
- Explain how you determined what **content and resources** to include and the factors that influenced your decisions (e.g. needs of students, interdisciplinary connections, availability of materials).
- Explain how you determined the **sequence** of the content and the activities in this unit.
- Describe how you determined when to **assess** and what to assess in this unit.
- Explain the **connection** between this unit and what followed.

Discuss the student artifact(s) you have provided from this unit. In your discussion:

- Explain **why** the artifact(s) was/were chosen.
- Discuss the artifact(s) in light of the **range of student responses** to the assigned work.
- Explain how the artifact(s) illustrates the **degree of persistence** the students demonstrated in producing it/them and their satisfaction with the completed product(s).
- Discuss how the artifact(s) was/were **assessed.**

Family Contact Log and Professional Development/School, Division, and Community Contribution Log

(Evidence of domain 4)

Discuss the logs or equivalent information you have kept. In your discussion:

- Explain your **record-keeping system** and the reasons for maintaining records in this manner.
- Explain the **types of contacts** you have had with your students' families and your reason for using these types of contacts.
- Summarize the professional development and other professionally-related activities in which you participated. Explain your contributions, as appropriate, and the **benefits** of this participation derived by you, the school and/or the division, and your students.

Note: If the teacher desires, any of these pieces of evidence may be submitted prior to June 1 and the conference on them held prior to the teacher's last contract day.

Summary of Evidence and Judgment of Performance

Reflect upon all the evidence that has been gathered by **both** the teacher and the assessor in all four domains. In your discussion:

- Describe how this collection illustrates the professional expectations for Newport News Public Schools teachers. Indicate in this discussion the level of performance this evidence represents (Unsatisfactory, Basic, Proficient, Distinguished).
- Discuss how the evidence collection relates to the Newport News Public Schools Teacher Performance Standards (meets, exceeds, does not meet division expectations).
- Discuss how this collection reflects the defining focus of Newport News Public Schools' mission, ". . . academic success for all students, regardless. . . ."

References

Archer, J. (1998, February 18). Students' fortune rests with assigned teacher. *Education Week, 9.*

Brophy, J. (1992). Probing the subtleties of subject-matter teaching. *Educational Leadership, 49,* 4–8.

Burke, K. (1997). *Designing professional portfolios for change.* Arlington Height, IL: IRI Skylight Publishing.

Chase, B. (1997, October 22). Teacher vs. Teacher? Nonsense. *Education Week, 26,* 29.

Conley, D. (1987). *Eight steps to improved teacher remediation.* Unpublished manuscript. Eugene: University of Oregon.

Danielson, C. (1996). *Enhancing professional practice: A framework for teaching.* Alexandria, VA: Association for Supervision and Curriculum Development.

Dietz, M. (1998). *Journals as frameworks for change.* Arlington Heights, IL: IRI Skylight Publishing.

Duke, D., & Stiggins, R. (1990). Beyond minimum competence: Evaluation for professional development. In J. Millman & L. Darling-Hammond (Eds.), *The new handbook of teacher evaluation.* Newbury Park, CA: Sage.

Eggen, P., & Kauchak, D. (1996). *Strategies for teachers: Teaching content and thinking skills.* Needham Heights, MA: Allyn & Bacon.

Haefele, D. L. (1993). Evaluating teachers: A call for change. *Journal of Personnel Evaluation in Education, 7,* 21–31.

Hawley, W., & Valli, L. (1999). The essentials of effective professional development: A new consensus. In L. Darling-Hammond & G. Sykes (Eds.), *Teaching as the learning profession: Handbook of policy and practice.* San Francisco: Jossey-Bass.

Haycock, K. (2000). Thinking K–16 report: Good teaching matters. [Online]. Washington, DC: The Education Trust. Available: http://www.edtrust.org

Hunter, M. C. (1982). *Mastery teaching.* Thousand Oaks, CA: Corwin Press.

Keillor, G. (1985). *Lake Wobegon days.* New York: Viking Penguin Inc.

Meux, M. (1974). Teaching the art of evaluating. *Journal of Aesthetic Education, 8*(1), 85.

Sanders, W. L., & Rivers, J. C. (1996, November). *Cumulative and residual effects of teachers on future student academic achievement.* Knoxville: University of Tennessee, Tennessee Value Added Assessment System (TVAAS). (Available from University of Tennessee, UTVARC, 225 Morgan Hall, P.O. Box 1071, Knoxville, TN 37901-1071).

Schon, D. A. (1983). *The reflective practitioner: How professionals think in action.* New York: Basic Books.

Schulman, L. (1997). Professing the liberal arts. In R. Orrill (Exec. Ed.), *Education and democracy: Re-imagining liberal learning in America.* New York: College Entrance Examination Board.

Scriven, M. (1988). Duty-based teacher evaluation. *Journal of Personnel Evaluation in Education, 1*(4), 319–334.

Scriven, M. (1994). The duties of the teacher. *Journal of Personnel Evaluation in Education, 8,* 151–184.

Wolf, K., Lichtenstein, G., & Stevenson, C. (1997). Using teaching portfolios in teacher evaluation. In J. Stronge (Ed.), *Teacher assessment and evaluation: A guide for research and practice.* Thousand Oaks, CA: Corwin Press.

Index

Note: Information contained in a figure is indicated by "(fig)" after the page number.

About the Authors

Charlotte Danielson, author of the 1996 ASCD book *Enhancing Professional Practice: A Framework for Teaching,* is an educational consultant in Princeton, New Jersey.

Phone: 609-683-0325
Fax: 609-683-8082
e-mail: charlotte_danielson@hotmail.com

Thomas L. McGreal is Professor Emeritus of Educational Organization and Leadership, University of Illinois at Champaign-Urbana. Contact him at 4009 Pinecrest Rd., Champaign, IL 61822.

Phone: 217-351-7379
e-mail: tmcgreal@uiuc.edu

Related ASCD Resources: Teacher Evaluation

Audiotapes

Building Brain-Based Schools, a live recording from the 1999 ASCD Annual Conference (stock no. 299089)

Evaluating Teachers in a Standards--Based Environment, live recording from the 1999 ASCD Annual Conference (stock no. 299158)

Portfolios: A Guide for Students and Teachers, 4-cassette audio pack (stock no. 299219)

Professional Portfolios: A Reflective and Performance Assessment Tool , live recording from the 1999 ASCD Annual Conference (stock no. 299113)

CD-ROMs

Curriculum Handbook on CD-ROM, 2nd Edition (1998; stock no. 598056)

Educational Leadership on CD-ROM (full text, 1994–1999; stock no. 598328)

Online Articles

Note: Go to the ASCD Web site (http://www.ascd.org) and search the "Reading Room" for these articles.

"New Goals for Teachers," by Larry Mann (*Education Update*, Vol. 41, No. 2 , March 1999)

"Policy Link: Pay for Performance," by Barbara Gleason (*Educational Leadership*, Vol. 57, No. 5, February 2000)

"Professional Development: The Linchpin of Teacher Quality," by Brian Sullivan (*Infobrief*, Issue 18, August 1999)

"Realizing the Promise of Standards--Based Education," by Mike Schmoker and Robert J. Marzano (*Educational Leadership*, Vol. 56, No. 6, March 1999)

"Teaching Worth Celebrating," by Patricia Wasley (*Educational Leadership*, Vol. 56, No. 8, May 1999)

"Using Rubrics to Promote Thinking and Learning," by Heidi Goodrich Andrade (*Educational Leadership*, Vol. 57, No. 5, February 2000)

Online Courses

Note: From the ASCD Web site (http://www.ascd.org), go to "Training Opportunities" and then to "Professional Development Online."

Effective Leadership (PD Online Course)

Systems Thinking (PD Online Course)

Print Products

ASCD Topic Pack—Teacher Evaluation /Teacher Portfolios (stock no. 197202)

A Better Beginning: Supporting and Mentoring New Teachers, edited by Marge Scherer (stock no. 199236)

Capturing the Wisdom of Practice: Professional Portfolios for Educators by Giselle O. Martin--Kniep (stock no. 199254)

Educators as Learners: Creating a Professional Learning Community in Your School, edited by Penelope J. Wald and Michael S. Castleberry (stock no. 100005)

Enhancing Professional Practice: A Framework for Teaching by Charlotte Danielson (stock no. 196074)

Improving Professional Performance, *Educational Leadership*, Vol. 53, No. 6, March 1996 (stock no. 196007)

Observing Dimensions of Learning in Classrooms and Schools by John L. Brown (stock no. 195209)

Real Questions, Real Answers: Focusing Teacher Leadership on School Improvement by John H. Clarke, Stephen D. Sanborn, Judith A. Aiken, Nancy A. Cornell, Jane Briody Goodman, and Karin K. Hess (stock no. 198007)

Standards for Excellence in Education: A Guide for Parents, Teachers, and Principals for Evaluating, by the Council for Basic Education (book stock no. 198338; kit stock no. 798339)

Teachers—Transforming Their World and Their Work by Ann Lieberman and Lynne Miller (stock no. 199217)

Videotapes

The Principal Series: Tape 6: The Principal as Instructional Leader (40 minute videotape plus Facilitator's Guide, stock no. 499240)

The Supervision Series: Another Set of Eyes (5 videotapes plus 2 trainers' manuals) by Keith Atcheson (stock no. 614179)

For additional resources, visit us on the World Wide Web (http://www.ascd.org), send an e-mail message to member@ascd.org, call the ASCD Service Center (1-800-933-ASCD or 703-578-9600, then press 2), send a fax to 703-575-5400, or write to Information Services, ASCD, 1703 N. Beauregard St., Alexandria, VA 22311-1714 USA.